rude food
nude food
good food

rude food
nude food
good food

JENNY MORRIS

The Giggling Gourmet

Human & Rousseau
Cape Town Pretoria Johannesburg

The Cape Talk team - Kieno

To my wonderful sons – from the top, Wade, Dann and Ryan – who always said I should write a cookbook. My darlings, this book is for you. I have been blessed with three wonderful sons, who share my passion.

To my husband, David, who is a nagger of note. When Marianne Nicol sowed the seed of a cookbook in his head, I never knew peace again. Just this one time, David, I have to thank you for nagging me.

To my wonderful friend Sue Nel, who taught me how to be organised while writing this book; I'm so glad I listened.

acknowledgements

Marianne it has been a pleasure to work with someone who is so talented, with such vision and a professional in every sense of the word.

To Abigail Donnelly – all pink and blonde, with the patience of a saint and a stunning sense of humour. Thank you for interpreting my food so beautifully.

To Dawie Verwey, my photographer; see, I told you that you would live through it all! Even if you never see a piece of fillet in the same light again, at least you will eat it with relish.

To John Binedell, my guinea pig who tasted his way through my book, thank you for your honest input.

And to my friends and colleagues at 567 CapeTalk Radio who have eaten, tasted and worked with me over the years – I love you all.

To Karen Pieters, thank you for being the best godmother and friend anyone could ask for, and for all the time you dedicated to my boys, while I was working on my book.

To David, I'm saying thank you again – I always say thank you, dear.

And finally, thank you, Marianne, for making it all happen.

First published in 2004 by Human & Rousseau
40 Heerengracht, Cape Town

10 9 8 7 6 5 4 3 2

Publisher: Marianne Nicol
Editor: Pat Barton
Designer: Chérie Collins
Photographer: Dawie Verwey
Stylist: Abigail Donnelly
Colour separation: Virtual Colour, Cape Town

ISBN 0 7981 4405 X

Printed in China through Colorcraft Ltd., Hong Kong
Props: LIM, Boardmans, Clicks, Weylandts, Heartworks,
The Yellow Door, The Plush Bazaar, Banks

contents

foreword

Jenny Morris has had an ongoing love affair with food since she was a child, when she started making mouth-watering treats for school fundraisers. It's a love affair in the true sense of the word; one which employs all the senses.

Taste and aroma are the most obvious, but for Jenny touch is also important. "Feeling your food is important," she says. "Caress it, stroke it, know it intimately." How you eat your food will reveal what kind of lover you are. "You don't want someone who eats a sosatie (kebab) with a knife and fork," says Jenny, with the naughty, spontaneous laugh that has earned her the moniker of Giggling Gourmet. "And if I can get presidents and heads of state to eat with their hands, I can get anyone to do it!" Among her kitchen essentials Jenny lists garlic, butter, olive oil, dhania (coriander) and her trusty zester [for making fine citrus strips]. "I simply cannot do without it. There is nothing better."

From these early beginnings, Jenny went on to cater for functions while she was at high school, and later cooked for friends and family. Besides running her own catering company, Jenny also teaches practical, hands-on cooking courses, which have fun and laughter as a main ingredient, at her cooking school. In December 1998, Jenny came under the media spotlight with a weekly food programme on Cape Talk radio (567Khz MW).

Her formula for success is to "entertain informatively and inform entertainingly", something she does with flair. Not only has she conquered radio but Jenny has also made several television appearances, both locally and internationally.

Jenny is much in demand at events such as food festivals, and makes regular appearances around the country. She is often commissioned by brand leaders to

demonstrate food and related products, is an examiner for The Culinary Academy, Cape Town, a judge for various food competitions, and accredited as an international judge for the International Barbeque Association. Jenny is much in demand as a celebrity chef, making appearances at a wider variety of functions and product launches.

A range of personally developed products that bear the Giggling Gourmet label – including Glaze 'n Baste™ and ChuckMe!™ sauces – can be found on selected deli shelves.

Although she has cooked for dozens of celebrities and royals, Jenny remains her down to earth self, and when she's not wowing the public she can be found in her kitchen stirring a pot of something fragrant and delicious. "Layer those flavours," she advises, "and feel that dish come alive in your hands."

For up-to-date information on what Jenny is up to, log on to the Giggling Gourmet website www.gigglinggourmet.com or e-mail Jenny at jennym@giggling-gourmet.com.

BIANCA COLEMAN
Food writer
The Argus

seduc-
tion

1

SEXY & SAUCY

STARTERS

Gingered Butternut Soup
Serves 6

15 ml (1 T) olive oil
2 ml (½ t) cumin seeds
3 slices fresh ginger
2 cloves garlic, crushed
1 stalk lemon grass, bashed
1 small red chilli, sliced (optional)
2 green cardamom pods
5 leeks, washed and sliced
30 ml (2 T) butter
1,5 kg butternut, peeled, seeded and cubed
2 green apples, with skin, chopped
grated zest of 1 orange
1 x 400 g can coconut cream
750 ml (3 c) long-life milk
125 ml (½ c) chopped fresh coriander

METHOD
1. Heat a heavy-based saucepan and add olive oil. Swirl to cover base of pan and add the ingredients, from the cumin seeds down to the leeks, stirring constantly.
2. Cook gently until the leeks have wilted, but take care not to let them brown.
3. Add the butter, butternut, apple and orange zest. Cook until the butternut is tender. If it becomes too dry, add just a little water to keep it moist. Now you can stir in the coconut cream.
4. Remove the lemon grass stalks and cardamom pods. It would be a sin to take the ginger out, but that's up to you.
5. Whack the mixture in a food processor until it's smooth, adding the milk gradually. Reheat, add the coriander and serve.

How to eat it
From a deep bowl, with chunks of freshly baked Peasant Bread (see recipe on page 62) for dunking. Slurping is a compliment to the chef.

seduction

How to choose the right butternut

It should have a very long neck – think ostrich or giraffe – with an ever-so-tiny bottom. That way you'll have lots and lots of flesh. And you'll save money too.

Big-bottomed butternuts are often hollow.

Red Pepper and Butter Bean Soup
Serves 6

4 red sweet peppers, cored and seeded
15 ml (1 T) butter
1 large onion, peeled and finely chopped
2 fat cloves garlic, crushed
2 ml (½ t) chilli powder
15 ml (1 T) tomato purée
2 x 425 g cans butter beans, drained
500 ml (2 c) chicken stock
salt and milled black pepper to taste
125 ml (½ c) roughly chopped fresh coriander
splash of fresh lemon juice and a drizzle of olive oil to serve

METHOD
1. Roast peppers (see recipe on page 49) and remove skins.
2. Heat the butter in a large saucepan, add onion and cook gently until translucent.
3. Stir in the garlic, chilli powder and tomato purée, and fry for a few minutes.
4. Add the beans, stir to coat with tomato purée, then add the chicken stock and simmer for 10 minutes, covered.
5. Add the sweet peppers, salt, pepper and coriander, and give it a good stir.
6. Purée until smooth, then reheat and serve with a splash of lemon juice and a drizzle of olive oil.

* Garnish with shaved parmesan, crispy bacon bits and roughly chopped Italian parsley.

Mushroom and Cream Cheese Soup, topped with Parmesan Toast

Serves 6

a little olive oil
10 g butter
1 onion, peeled and finely chopped
500 g mixed mushrooms, wiped and sliced
2 stalks celery, trimmed and sliced
5 ml (1 t) dried oregano
1 clove fresh garlic, chopped
salt and milled black pepper
500 ml (2 c) chicken or vegetable stock
1 x 250 g tub green onion cream cheese
ciabatta
grated Parmesan cheese

METHOD

1. Heat a little olive oil and the butter and gently fry the onion, mushrooms, celery stalks, oregano and garlic. Season with salt and pepper to taste.
2. Add the stock and simmer for 10 minutes.
3. Purée with green onion cream cheese.
4. Slice ciabatta and paint with olive oil. Top with Parmesan cheese.
5. Place under a preheated grill until the cheese melts. Serve soup topped with slices of Parmesan toast.

Persian Soup
Serves 10

When you get one of those plump sultanas, your mouth will love you.

2 litres (8 c) Greek yoghurt
2 bunches spring onions, trimmed, roots discarded, and onions chopped
250 ml (1 c) roughly chopped walnuts
1 large cucumber, grated and drained
8 hard-boiled eggs, peeled and chopped
4 cloves garlic, crushed
500 ml (2 c) sultanas
125 ml (½ c) chopped fresh mint
salt and milled black or white pepper
250 ml (1 c) cream

METHOD
1. Line a strainer with muslin and peg it down to secure it.
2. Pour in the yoghurt and strain out the liquid until the yoghurt is nice and thick.
3. Place the yoghurt in a glass bowl. Add the spring onions, walnuts, cucumber, eggs, garlic, sultanas, mint, salt and pepper and mix well.
4. Refrigerate for 24 hours.
5. Stir in the cream and chill until ready to serve.
6. Dust with paprika and serve with crosti.

* This soup will keep for a maximum of 3 days.
* You can add more garlic if you wish.

Smoked Fish Pâté
Serves 10 as a snack, with Melba toast.

500 g potatoes, peeled and boiled
125 ml (½ c) warm milk
salt and milled black pepper
3 cloves garlic, crushed
500 g smoked angelfish, boned, skinned, flaked
freshly chopped Italian parsley
125 ml (½ c) olive oil

METHOD
1. Mash the potatoes, adding the milk, salt, pepper and garlic.
2. Add the fish and parsley, then beat in the olive oil. Taste and adjust the seasoning if necessary. If it is too stiff, add more olive oil to get a smooth consistency.

* When a recipe calls for black pepper, the pepper should be freshly milled so that the flavour is fresh, hot and penetrating.

Chicken Liver Pâté
Serves 6

Make this pâté 24 hours before you need it.

1 onion, peeled and chopped
100 g butter
1 kg chicken livers
125 ml (½ c) sherry
10 ml (2 t) dried tarragon
10 ml (2 t) brandy
salt and milled black pepper
2 cloves garlic
250 ml (1 c) fresh cream

METHOD
1. Fry the onion in the heated butter until translucent.
2. Add the livers and brown lightly on all sides (they must still be pink inside).
3. Add the sherry, tarragon, brandy, salt and pepper.
4. Simmer for 10 minutes, then remove from the heat.
5. Purée the livers and garlic until smooth. Add cream and purée until smooth.
6. Pour into a dish and allow to cool down.
7. When cold, cover and place in fridge to set. Serve with Melba toast.

* I like to use Old Brown Sherry in this dish, it gives a lovely nutty flavour.

Potted Soft Cheese Pâté
Serves 8

This keeps hunger at bay while everyone is waiting for those juicy steaks to come off the BBQ.

```
200 g feta cheese
250 g cream cheese
2 cloves garlic, crushed
15 ml (1 T) chopped fresh mint
15 ml (1 T) chopped fresh dill
250 ml (1 c) roughly chopped rocket
250 ml (1 c) roughly chopped Italian parsley
milled black pepper
125 ml (½ c) pesto
250 ml (1 c) Rosa tomatoes, roasted (see recipe on page 44)
250 ml (1 c) toasted pine nuts
```

METHOD
1. Mix the feta, cream cheese, garlic, herbs and pepper together lightly.
2. Spray a small bowl with nonstick cooking spray and line it with cling film.
3. Pack in the cheese mixture, cover and refrigerate overnight.
4. Unmould onto a plate, remove the cling film and top the cheese mixture with pesto, roasted tomatoes and pine nuts. Serve with special breads and salad.

* Leave out the salad and serve with water biscuits or crostini.
* I like to ring the changes by using goat's milk cheese instead of feta.

seduction

Camembert Lunch
Serves 4

This is great to serve with drinks while someone is firing up the braai.

1 x 250 g firm, not yet ripe Camembert, preferably Dalewood
30 ml (2 T) pesto
45 ml (3 T) toasted pine nuts
3 pears, thinly sliced

METHOD
1. Split the Camembert horizontally.
2. Lightly spread pesto on bottom half, then add toasted pine nuts and thin slices of pear.
3. Close with the top half. Serve with hot Italian bread.

* Now for a great mouth moment: Top a very ripe Dalewood Brie or Camembert with the pesto, pine nuts and pear slices and tuck in. I love the way the centre just oozes out all over the plate.
* In fact, forget the topping and take a ripe cheese, a bottle of red and two glasses to bed with you, and dig into the cheese with your fingers.

Hot Camembert and Fig Preserve
Serves 4-6

This is so rich that you could even serve 8.

1 firm, not yet ripe Camembert, preferably Dalewood
250 ml (1 c) mascarpone cheese
100 g Gorgonzola-style blue cheese
chopped walnuts
sliced preserved figs
honey

METHOD
1. Preheat the oven to 200 °C.
2. Split the cheese horizontally and layer mascarpone, blue cheese, and half the walnuts and preserved figs on the bottom half.
3. Close with the top half, then drizzle with honey and top with the remaining nuts and preserved figs.
4. Bake for 5 minutes and serve.

Green Asparagus with Pork Fillet Wraparounds and an Asian Dipping Sauce

Serves 4

The quantities given for the sauce are merely intended to be a guide. So trust your taste buds, take the recipe and own it.

1 pork fillet
salt and milled black pepper
fresh green asparagus spears, blanched and refreshed
oil

SAUCE
250 ml (1 c) Indonesian sweet soy sauce
125 ml (½ c) rice vinegar
1 clove garlic, crushed
125 ml (½ c) pickled ginger
1 red chilli (optional)

METHOD
1. Cut the pork fillet into thin slices.
2. Gently beat the slices to flatten them lightly. Season with salt and pepper.
3. Place 1 asparagus on each slice of pork and roll up.
4. Whizz all the sauce ingredients together in a blender. This keeps for weeks – if you have anything left.
5. Heat the oil in a pan and fry wraparounds quickly on all sides, but don't overcook.
6. Arrange on a platter and drizzle with sauce.
7. Pour the remaining sauce into a bowl for dipping.

* Can be used as finger food, or as a plated starter, or even served with wilted greens and noodles as a main course.
* This is such a sexy dish – watch how the girls eat them; the tip always goes into the mouth first. The boys seem to bite the bottom off first! It's true, believe me. I've studied this.

How to buy asparagus
Always choose spears with tightly closed heads and slender, crisp stems.

Balsamic Onions
Serves as many as you want

The longer these onions stand, the better they taste! It's rather pleasant to keep one in your cheek to suck out all that lovely balsamic syrup …

peeled pickling onions
olive oil to drizzle
salt
crushed garlic

DRESSING
fresh garlic, crushed
honey, to taste
balsamic vinegar, to taste
5 ml (1 t) whole-grain mustard

METHOD
1. Preheat the oven to 180 °C.
2. Mix together the onions, olive oil, salt and garlic and place in an ovenproof dish.
3. Roast until golden brown but still firm.
4. Shake all the dressing ingredients together.
5. Toss onions with dressing and leave to marinate for 24 hours, or longer.

A little balsamic tip
If you are using a young balsamic vinegar, pour it into a large basin and let it evaporate a little and it won't be so acidic.

seduction

fore-play

2

SCRUMPTIOUS SALADS
& ALMOST NAKED
VEGETABLES

One of my earliest memories of food goes back to when I was about three years old – I know I was that young, because my grandpa Bob was still alive and we lived in the cottage in the grounds of Holly Villa, at 235 Avondale Road in Durban, South Africa.

I can remember being in the kitchen of my parents' home and hearing a little snap and a crunching sound – I looked up to see my father with a salt cellar and this beautiful green stick in his hand. He was shaking salt on the green stick and biting it. The look of satisfaction on his face as he chewed made my mouth water … when I asked him what it was, he said I was too young to try it. If only he knew what a nagging craving he created inside me! To this day, celery is one of my favourite vegetable snacks.

My grandpa Bob would call me for tea every afternoon; he used to make fresh, light crumpets for tea. I can still see and taste them: light as air, with blobs of melting butter and honey.

He had a mandarin tree in his garden. The fruit had a green skin, the fattest segments I've ever seen and the most marvellous flavour, one that is imprinted in my memory bank. I would open the membrane, break up the fat juicy cells and pop a few at a time in my mouth … and let them burst to release the sweet, sweet juice. When my grandparents died, we moved into the Big House and that mandarin tree became mine.

My father planted a Hanepoot grapevine that didn't bear much fruit. I can remember how excited he was when it bore its first bunch of grapes; he would lift the leaves every night and talk to the grapes. When they started to ripen the temptation became too great: I plucked one from the back of the bunch, and as my teeth broke through the skin the sweet flavours filled my mouth. I longed to have more, but my guilt and terror stopped me. When dad checked the precious bunch that night, he never noticed that one of the grapes was missing. I relaxed. But the memory of that flavour stayed with me, and the next day I sat behind the gardener's house, savouring the grapes one by one. When my dad discovered the bare stem, he was beside himself. He threatened to punish the one responsible for eating his grapes, but luckily for me, the truth never came out.

When I was seven we sold the house to a property developer who wanted to build blocks of flats. I cried and cried because he was going to uproot my beautiful mandarin tree. We moved to Pinetown, to a huge property that my father filled with every fruit and vegetable imaginable.

When I got home from school, I would put down my school bag, grab the salt cellar and make my way, with my sister Beverley, to the garden for lunch.

Lunch was everything straight from the plant: Green peppers – you can't imagine the flavour, texture and crunch; baby sugar loaf cabbages, baby cucumbers, tomatoes, green beans, the sweetest peas in their pods … all of them as fresh as could be. Our gardener, Pharaoh (who hated me, but adored my brother Billy), would complain bitterly that I was murdering the babies before they were big enough to eat.

I wonder if any of my dad's friends remember that garden? They would come to visit, carrying a sack in their hands and leave with it full.

My mother, who is now 77, and my step-dad, who is in his eighties, still grow everything they eat, and work their land without help. I'm convinced that my mother's good health and energy come from eating vegetables raw or al dente; never soaking anything in water for hours, letting all the goodness leach out.

My love affair with fresh food started when I was very young and continues to this day. I can still remember the crunchiness and flavour of those vegetables fresh from the garden, and my mouth has never forgotten what my mother taught me about fresh.

Thai Pineapple and Baby Bean Salad
Serves 6-8

1 ripe pineapple, peeled and cut into chunks
200 g baby green beans, blanched and refreshed*
4 carrots, peeled and julienned
250 ml (1 c) Turkish dried apricots, soaked in water and drained
250 ml (1 c) roughly chopped dried mango
2 cloves garlic, crushed
250 ml (1 c) roughly chopped coriander
125 ml (½ c) sweet piquanté pepper sauce
125 ml (½ c) pineapple juice
splash of lime juice

METHOD
1. Fling the lot into a bowl 24 hours before you want to eat it.
2. Cover and refrigerate.
3. Keep turning the fruit and vegetables to coat them in the juices.
4. Take out 1 hour before serving. The juices will have mingled to make a dressing.

* Refreshing the blanched beans in ice-cold water will ensure that they stay green and crisp.
* If you can't find Turkish apricots, use local dried ones instead.

Indonesian Sweet Soy Salad
Serves 8-10

I love ginger – whether it is fresh, pickled or preserved in a thick syrup, so if you feel the same way add more ginger!

```
4 carrots, julienned
100 g mangetout, topped and tailed
100 g baby green beans, topped and tailed and blanched
1 red sweet pepper, cored, seeded and sliced
1 yellow sweet pepper, cored, seeded and sliced
1 bunch of radishes, washed and thickly sliced
1 punnet baby corn
250 ml (1 c) cauliflower florets
1 punnet fresh bean sprouts
```

```
DRESSING
250 ml (1 c) Indonesian sweet soy sauce
125 ml (½ c) chopped pickled ginger, with some of the juice
125 ml (½ c) olive oil
3 cloves garlic, crushed
```

METHOD
1. Shake all the dressing ingredients together.
2. Toss all the vegetables, except the cauliflower and sprouts, in the dressing.
3. Leave to stand for 2 days.
4. Add the cauliflower and sprouts on the day you eat the salad (otherwise every time you open the fridge you'll have to say, "It's not me!"). Keep turning the vegetables to coat them in the dressing.

Rice Pasta Salad
Serves 8-10

Okay, lazy, the beans can be canned – the kidney beans and the chickpeas, that is, but definitely not the green beans.

250 ml (1 c) olive oil
juice of 2 lemons
500 ml (2 c) uncooked rice pasta (orzo)
250 ml (1 c) pitted black olives
250 ml (1 c) chopped sundried tomatoes
250 ml (1 c) roughly chopped Italian parsley
250 ml (1 c) cooked chickpeas
250 ml (1 c) red kidney beans
250 ml (1 c) roughly chopped blanched green beans (see page 33)
2 fresh garlic cloves, crushed
1 red chilli, sliced (optional)
salt and milled black pepper
250 ml (1 c) wild or ordinary rocket
shavings of fresh Parmesan cheese

METHOD
1. Mix the olive oil and lemon juice in a bowl. Toss everything, except the rocket and Parmesan cheese, in the mixture.
2. Marinate for at least 2 hours, but preferably 4.
3. Add the rocket and fling the lot together. Let it stand for 1 hour.
4. Top with Parmesan shavings and serve.

* Gently rinse the brine off the canned beans and chickpeas for a better flavour.

Wild Rice Salad
Serves 8

When I talk about chopped spring onions in my recipes, the entire onion, except the root, is used.

250 ml (1 c) wild rice
250 ml (1 c) brown rice
1 punnet baby leeks, thinly sliced
2 red sweet peppers roasted and cut into strips (see recipe on
  page 49)
250 ml (1 c) sultanas
250 ml (1 c) roughly chopped Italian parsley, plus extra for
  garnishing
250 ml (1 c) toasted cashew nuts
125 ml (½ c) toasted pine nuts
1 bunch spring onions, chopped
3 cloves garlic, crushed
190 ml (¾ c) olive oil
juice of 1 lemon
salt and milled pepper to taste
200 g haloumi cheese, cubed

METHOD
1. Cook the rice separately until al dente, wash and drain.
2. Deep-fry the leeks in batches and add to the rice.
3. Now mix everything together, except the haloumi cheese.
4. Cover and leave in the fridge for 24 hours.
5. When you are ready to serve, deep-fry cubes of haloumi cheese and scatter them over the salad with more chopped parsley.
6. Adjust the seasoning, if necessary; you might want more lemon juice.

* I toast my nuts in a dry frying pan, keep them seperate as some take longer to toast than others. Toasting enhances the flavour.

Fresh Fennel Salad
Serves 6

2 fennel bulbs, thinly sliced
1 red onion, peeled and thinly sliced
salt and milled black pepper
1 punnet baby Bella tomatoes, halved
250 ml (1 c) roughly chopped Italian parsley
30 ml (2 T) capers
1 clove garlic, crushed
olive oil

METHOD
1. Mix sliced fennel and onion together.
2. Salt the vegetables and leave to sweat for at least 30 minutes.
3. Add the tomatoes, chopped parsley and capers, black pepper, garlic and olive oil.
4. Now, using your hands, gently pull the flavours together. Feel that food!
5. Let the mixture rest in the fridge for at least 2 hours before eating.

How to eat it
* Add 100 g goat's milk cheese and serve on warm bruschetta drizzled with olive oil, or stuff it in pita bread.
* Chop a small can of anchovies, add to the mixture and use as a topping for poached fish or chicken breasts. Don't forget to splash with the juice of 1 lemon for extra zing.
* Toss with couscous and a squeeze of lemon juice.

Now I'm tired of making suggestions, take the recipe and own it!

How to buy fennel
When buying fennel make sure it has a wonderful rounded bulb, curvaceous like a woman's bottom.

foreplay

Hot Grilled Fruit Salad
Serves 8

Perfect for brunch or dessert.

1 pineapple, peeled and cut into chunks
3 nectarines, cut into quarters
3 oranges, peeled and thickly sliced
2 Granny Smith apples, cored and thickly sliced
2 pears, quartered, but with skin, pips and stem intact
1 whole red chilli
250 ml (1 c) cream
good dusting of ground cinnamon
100 g butter, cubed
lots of honey

METHOD
1. Preheat the oven to 220 °C.
2. Place the fruit and chilli in a roasting pan.
3. Pour over the cream, dust with cinnamon and toss together.
4. Dot with butter and drizzle lightly with honey.
5. Whack into the oven and bake until the fruit is cooked but still firm and the sauce is bubbling and fudgy, about 15 minutes. Serve hot.

Turkish Apricot and Nut Salad
Serves 6

100 g feta cheese, broken into chunks
250 ml (1 c) roughly chopped Turkish apricots
250 ml (1 c) rocket
250 ml (1 c) halved pecan nuts
125 ml (½ c) toasted sunflower seeds
1 bunch spring onions, sliced

250 ml (1 c) sultanas soaked in water until plump, then drained
2 cloves garlic, crushed
125 ml (½ c) olive oil
2 apples, peeled, cored and diced
shaved Parmesan cheese

METHOD
1. Mix all the ingredients, except the Parmesan cheese, together lightly.
2. Garnish the salad with Parmesan shavings and serve.

* Add chopped roast chicken for a non-vegetarian option.

New Potato Salad with Walnuts, Bacon and Other Tasty Things
Serves 6

This salad is really good. If you have the budget, use 250 ml (1 c) pine nuts and 125 ml (½ c) walnuts.

500 g new potatoes, steamed in their skins
1 bunch spring onions, finely chopped
salt and lots of milled black pepper
125 ml (½ c) roughly chopped Italian parsley
1 clove garlic, crushed
250 ml (1 c) fresh cream
250 g streaky bacon, chopped and crisply fried
250 ml (1 c) home-made mayonnaise or a good bought one
250 ml (1 c) wild or ordinary rocket
250 ml (1 c) roughly chopped toasted walnuts
125 ml (½ c) toasted pine nuts

METHOD
1. Cut potatoes in half.
2. Sprinkle the spring onions with 2 ml (½ t) salt and let them stand for ½ hour. Don't throw away the juice that develops as this adds lots of flavour.
3. Toss everything together, except the mayonnaise, rocket and nuts.
4. Add the mayonnaise to the salad and season. Set aside, covered, for 1 hour.
5. Stir in the rocket and nuts. Enjoy.

* Substitute sundried tomatoes for the bacon. Add the juice of ½ lemon if your mayonnaise comes out of a bottle.
* If you can't get wild rocket, ordinary will do. Chop it roughly.
* Always chop parsley stems and add them to the dish. Don't you dare throw them away!

To toast nuts
Place them in a hot, dry frying pan and stir over heat for a few minutes. Do not allow to burn. Toasting makes all the difference to the flavour.

Red Onion, Mango and Rocket Salad
Serves 4-5

I know I don't have to tell you what to do with the mango pips … but do find a quiet corner to indulge! Better still, buy an extra mango – choose a large one – and bite into its firm, thick flesh. Take in the heavenly perfume, let the flavour explode in your mouth and let the juices run down your chin.

3 large firm ripe mangoes, peeled
2 red onions, peeled and thinly sliced
salt and lots of milled black pepper
2 handfuls of rocket
2 cloves garlic, crushed
65 ml (¼ c) olive oil
juice of 1 large lemon

METHOD
1. Slice the mangoes quite thickly.
2. Put the onions in a glass dish, salt them and let them stand for 1 hour. We want the juice, so keep it and add for lots of flavour.
3. Mix the onions, rocket, mangoes, garlic, olive oil and lemon juice together. Give the mixture a good grinding of black pepper.
4. Toss all the ingredients together gently with your hands. Lick your fingers. Now wash your hands.
5. Refrigerate the salad until you are ready to eat.

Roasted Rosa Tomatoes
Serves 4

1 small punnet Rosa tomatoes
crushed garlic
rock salt
1 sprig rosemary
olive oil

METHOD
1. Preheat the oven to 200 °C.
2. Toss all the ingredients together.
3. Transfer to a shallow baking pan and roast until the skins burst but tomatoes are still intact, about 10 minutes.

foreplay

Asian Seared Fillet of Beef Salad
Serves 4

The fillet should be rare and juicy; in fact it should scream, "Eat me!"

600 g beef fillet
olive oil
salt and milled white pepper
30 ml (2 T) toasted sesame seeds

SALAD
100 g very young green beans, blanched and refreshed (see page 33)
500 ml (2 c) bean sprouts
1 red onion, peeled and thinly sliced
fresh coriander to taste
½ bunch radishes, thinly sliced

METHOD
1. Rub the fillet with olive oil. Season with salt and pepper.
2. Heat a little oil to piping hot in a heavy-based frying pan. Sear the fillet on all sides.
3. Remove from the stove and set aside to rest before slicing.
4. Toss all the salad ingredients together and divide between 4 plates.
5. Top with sliced fillet and spoon over Asian Dipping Sauce (see recipe on page 26).
6. Sprinkle with sesame seeds and enjoy.

* Don't use spongy radishes; choose small, firm, crisp ones and use the whole bunch.
* I often arrange this salad on a large platter and add it to a buffet.

Mushrooms and Artichokes
Serves 6

Great as a starter. Most of us don't eat enough raw mushrooms – they're delicious,
packed with goodness and really low in fat (leaves room for more BUTTER).
If you eat a lot of low-kilojoule mushrooms, you can have any dish without guilt.
Make the salad a day ahead, so that it has time to mature.

1 kg of the freshest, whitest, tightest button mushrooms you can find,
  wiped (don't ever wash!) and halved
2 x 410 g cans artichoke hearts, drained

DRESSING
5 ml (1 t) salt
75 ml (5 T) coriander seeds
250 ml (1 c) red wine vinegar
250 ml (1 c) olive oil
4 cloves garlic, crushed
375 ml (1½ c) roughly chopped Italian parsley

METHOD
1. First make the dressing. Place the salt, coriander seeds and wine vinegar in a
   saucepan.
2. Bring to the boil and cook, uncovered, over high heat until it reduces to about
   15 ml (1 T) liquid. Remove from the stove.
3. Add olive oil and garlic and give it a stir.
4. Pull (gently fold) half the parsley through the mushrooms and the other half
   through the artichokes. [I'm watching you: are you using your hands?]
5. Arrange the mushrooms in the bottom of your dish. Now pour the dressing over
   the artichokes and gently mix it in, using your hands.
6. Put the artichokes on top of the mushrooms and cover.
7. After 6 hours, gently mix the mushrooms and artichokes together, using your
   hands.

* Every time I bite into one of those little coriander seeds I get excited – try it!

Roasted Peppers
Serves 1

Make as many roasted peppers as you wish; remember that 1 pepper will feed 1 person.

1 red sweet pepper
olive oil

METHOD
1. Cut the pepper into 4.
2. Remove pips and pith.
3. Place on a baking sheet and drizzle with olive oil.
4. Place under the grill until lightly charred and blistered.
5. Remove from oven, place in a glass bowl and cover with a plate – let the steam do the work for you and loosen the skins.
6. Peel off the skin, save the juice and use as desired.

* If you come across a piece of stubborn skin, use a toothpick to slide under the skin to loosen it.

Baby Beets with a Balsamic Vinegar, Honey and Oregano Drizzle
Serves 4-6

I'm sure not crazy about skin on a sausage, don't mind it on nuts although I'd rather have it off, but darling it would be a sin to remove the skin from vegetables! That's where all the flavour and good stuff is. It adds colour and texture.

3 baby beets per person, stem and root intact, lightly steamed (you can leave the skins on too; all the goodness lies beneath the skin)

DRESSING
375 ml (1½ c) balsamic vinegar
2 cloves garlic, crushed
45 ml (3 T) soy sauce
125 ml (½ c) honey - more if you like
125 ml (½ c) chopped fresh oregano

METHOD
1. Pour balsamic vinegar and garlic into a saucepan.
2. Boil briskly over high heat, uncovered, until reduced by half.
3. Add the soy sauce and honey and cook for 2 minutes.
4. Remove from the heat, add oregano and stir.

How to eat it
Place the beets in the centre of each plate. Drizzle with dressing and twirl the baby beet in the dressing. Suck the dressing off the root, bite off and eat the root, then dip and eat until you reach the stem – that tastes good too. Enjoy the earthy sweetness of this wonderful vegetable!

foreplay

Brinjal Slices stuffed with Ricotta, wrapped in Spinach and baked in two Sauces
Serves 6

6 long, firm brinjals with firm, tight bottoms
olive oil
24 large spinach leaves, blanched and spines removed
grated Parmesan cheese
Red Pepper Sauce (see recipe on page 156)
Cheese Sauce (see recipe on page 157)

RICOTTA STUFFING
500 g ricotta cheese
2 cloves garlic, crushed
75 ml (5 T) chopped Italian parsley
45 ml (3 T) pine nuts
90 ml (6 T) grated Parmesan cheese
salt and white pepper

METHOD
This dish can be assembled before the time and baked just before serving.
1. Cut each brinjal into 4 lengthways slices. Sprinkle with salt and leave to sweat for 30 minutes. Rinse and pat dry.
2. Heat a little olive oil in a frying pan and fry the brinjal slices gently on both sides, until lightly coloured. Drain on absorbent paper.
3. Mix all the stuffing ingredients together and place in the fridge.
4. Preheat the oven to 180 °C.
5. Lay out the brinjal slices on a clean working surface, top with the ricotta mixture and roll each one up.
6. Lay out the spinach leaves, top each with a brinjal roll-up and wrap into neat, sausage-like parcels.
7. Pack the parcels into a buttered heatproof dish, top with Red Pepper Sauce, then with Cheese Sauce and sprinkle Parmesan cheese over.
8. Bake for 25 minutes, or until bubbling.
9. Serve with salad and garlic bread.

* Ricotta is an exceptionally versatile cheese; it can be used as filling in pasta dishes and pastries, and is great drizzled with olive oil and baked.

Alma's Green Beans, Pecan Nuts and Sherry
Serves 6

My mother-in-law always used to double this recipe, because I just could not get enough. Oh, those nuts … what the heck, add an extra handful!

1 kg baby green beans, topped and tailed
250 ml (1 c) roughly chopped pecan nuts

DRESSING
30 ml (2 T) brown sugar
125 ml (½ c) soy sauce
250 ml (1 c) old brown sherry
3 cloves garlic, crushed
250 ml (1 c) olive oil

METHOD
1. Blanch the beans and refresh in iced water (see page 33). Drain and dry.
2. Make the dressing. Mix the sugar, soy sauce, sherry and garlic, and stir until the sugar dissolves.
3. Add the olive oil and shake together well.
4. Mix the beans and nuts. Pour the dressing over, cover and leave to soak up the flavours for 2 days.

Apples and Sweet Potatoes with Honey and Ginger
Serves 6

Fresh, warm and fragrant ginger has a wonderful bite. Nature's Viagra is good for your circulation; it keeps the blood flowing to all those special places.

3 large, crunchy Granny Smith apples
3 large, firm sweet potatoes
1 cm piece fresh ginger, peeled and grated
salt and milled black pepper
2 cloves garlic, crushed
2 ml (½ t) ground cloves
2 ml (½ t) ground cinnamon
olive oil
honey
75 ml (5 T) butter

METHOD
1. Preheat the oven to 180 °C.
2. Core and slice the apples thickly. Scrub the sweet potatoes, slice them thickly.
3. Place the apples, sweet potatoes, ginger, salt and pepper, garlic, cloves and cinnamon in a large bowl.
4. Lace with olive oil and mix well to coat.
5. Place the sweet potatoes in an ovenproof dish, drizzle with honey and dot with butter, then add the apples.
6. Dot with butter and drizzle with honey.
7. Bake until golden and cooked through. Serve with roast pork.

How to choose ginger
Fresh ginger should be heavy, hard, plump and unwrinkled.

Sweet Potatoes roasted with Garlic, Chilli and Rosemary

Serves 6

I always try to find the violet-coloured sweet potatoes, but the pink-skinned ones are great too.

4 long, firm violet- or pink-skinned sweet potatoes, well-scrubbed
6 cloves garlic, roughly chopped
5 red chillies
lots of rosemary, fresh of course!
coarse salt and milled black pepper
olive oil
10 ml (2 t) dark brown sugar
fresh coriander

METHOD

1. Preheat the oven to 180 °C.
2. Slice the sweet potatoes into thick rings, or cut them into wedges or chunks. (Whatever you do, don't peel them!)
3. Place the sweet potatoes, garlic, chillies and rosemary in a bowl.
4. Season with salt and pepper, and don't be shy with the olive oil; give them a good dousing, using your hands.
5. Flip the sweet potatoes all around to coat with the mixture.
6. Pop the sweet potatoes into a roasting pan, sprinkle with brown sugar and bake until sticky, golden and soft.
7. Garnish with fresh coriander and enjoy.

Buying sweet potatoes

Sweet potatoes (Ipomoea batatas) are full of flavour, and have lots of fibre. The yellow-fleshed ones contain beta-carotene. Buy them fresh, really firm, with no blemishes or smells. And if you are going to roast them, simply scrub them gently (do not peel).

Gingered Carrots
Serves 4-6

The carrots should retain some crunch

olive oil
500 g carrots, scraped and julienned
5 ml (1 t) ground ginger
olive oil for stir-frying
45 ml (3 T) honey
75 ml (5 T) butter

METHOD
1. Heat a little olive oil in a frying pan, add the carrots and ginger and stir-fry for about 7 minutes.
2. Add the honey and toss to coat carrots well.
3. Add the butter. Increase the heat and continue stir-frying for a minute or two.
4. Remove the carrots from the pan and cook the butter mixture over high heat, uncovered, until syrupy. Return carrots to the frying pan and reheat before serving.

sur-render

SOMETHING ON THE SIDE & INNOVATIVE QUICKIES

I love informal meals; they can be as long or short as you like and you can include as many dishes as you wish. A good cook is brave and original. Remember all those true sayings: a little bit of this and that never hurt anybody, variety is the spice of life … excite all the senses with the colours, textures and smells of your Groaning Table.

Karen's Pasta
Serves 6

My friend Karen is crazy about this dish – this one's for you, Karen!

100 g bacon, chopped
15 ml (1 T) butter
250 ml (1 c) chopped mushrooms
3 fat cloves garlic, crushed
1 bunch spring onions, chopped
250 ml (1 c) sundried tomatoes
500 ml (2 c) cream
125 ml (½ c) torn basil
65 ml (¼ c) fresh coriander
250 ml (1 c) freshly grated Parmesan cheese
salt and milled black pepper
500 g penne rigate, cooked al dente
125 ml (½ c) toasted macadamia nuts
125 ml (½ c) toasted cashew nuts
125 ml (½ c) toasted pine nuts

METHOD
1. Fry the bacon until crisp and remove it from the pan.
2. Add the butter, mushrooms, garlic, spring onions and sundried tomatoes to the pan and cook, stirring, for about 8 minutes.
3. Add the cream and cook until it is reduced and clings to the mushrooms.
4. Add the basil, coriander, Parmesan cheese, salt to taste and lots of black pepper.
5. Stir into the cooked penne with the nuts, and serve.

* Always add fresh herbs right at the end of cooking, so that you will capture every drop of flavour the volatile oil has to give.
* Toasting the nuts releases all the nutty oils and flavour and provides extra crunch.

Pasta with Blue Cheese, Peppercorns and Bacon
Serves 6

My wonderful, crazy, red-headed friend, Antoinette de Chavonnes-Vrugt, who never sleeps, served me this divine pasta one day … and I had to take her recipe and own it. So here it is, with my twist.

250 ml (1 c) chopped bacon, fried
250 g mascarpone cheese
200 g blue cheese
2 cloves garlic, crushed
125 ml (½ c) cream
30 ml (2 T) Madagascar green peppercorns, or more
500 g penne pasta, cooked al dente
salt and milled black pepper to taste

METHOD
1. Whack the whole lot, except the peppercorns, pasta and seasoning, in a saucepan, over moderate heat.
2. Wait for the meltdown, stirring occasionally. When the mixture is smooth and creamy, add the peppercorns, then add the pasta and toss until well covered.
3. Check the seasoning and serve.

How to eat it
Hot! The peppercorns will pop in your mouth – an unexpectedly pleasant surprise, a bit like an orgasm. If you get more than one peppercorn, you can brag that you've had a multiple orgasm!

Peasant Bread
Serves 10

Instant yeast put bread on my table – it is really so easy to use.

1,5 litres (6 c) cake flour
10 ml (2 t) salt
20 ml (4 t) sugar
10 g instant dried yeast
125 ml (½ c) chopped fresh rosemary
350-500 ml (⅖-2 c) lukewarm water
20 ml (4 t) olive oil
125 ml (½ c) pitted black olives
rosemary sprigs and black olives to garnish
olive oil mixed with water to glaze

METHOD
1. Put all the dry ingredients in the bowl of an electric mixer with a dough hook, and give it a twirl to mix.
2. Fling in the rosemary, turn on the mixer and start adding the liquid and oil alternately until the mixture starts to hold together.
3. Add the chopped olives to the mixture with the rest of the oil.
4. Knead, using the dough hooks, until smooth and elastic to the touch. Remove from the bowl.
5. Oil the dough lightly, place in a bowl, cover and leave to rise to twice its size.
6. Remove from the bowl, place on a greased baking sheet and shape the loaf as desired.
7. Make shallow diagonal slashes in the dough and poke in some rosemary and olives.
8. Brush with olive oil and water glaze.
9. Allow to rise again to twice its size.
10. Preheat the oven to 200 °C.
11. Bake the loaf for 20–25 minutes, or until it sounds hollow when tapped.
12. Cool on a cooling rack.

* Never mix instant yeast with water; always add it to the flour, then add the liquid.
* Add the water a little at a time, not all at once, as different brands of flour have different absorption rates. Remember: you can add water, but you can't take it away.

Hot Mushroom Sandwich
Serves 4

I'd serve everything in bed if I could, but this one is best served on a bed of beautifully fresh baby greens.

```
250 g mixed sliced mushrooms
2 cloves garlic, chopped
6 spring onions, trimmed and chopped
50 ml (⅕ c) butter
5 ml (1 t) sesame oil
30 ml (2 T) chopped chives
30 ml (2 T) roughly chopped Italian parsley
100 g rocket
1 large ciabatta loaf, sliced diagonally
250 g cream cheese
lots of salad leaves
250 ml (1 c) cherry tomatoes, cut in half lengthways
```

METHOD
1. Stir-fry the mushrooms, garlic and spring onions in heated butter and sesame oil.
2. Remove the frying pan from the heat and stir in the herbs.
3. Grill the ciabatta.
4. Toss the mushrooms into the cream cheese, mixing lightly, and reserve a blob for garnish.
5. Pile onto ciabatta slices and serve on a bed of salad greens and halved cherry tomatoes.

How to buy rocket

Choose crisp young leaves that are fresh and unblemished, then savour the delicious, peppery flavour. A packet of rocket seeds will go a very long way in your garden.

Mushroom Risotto
Serves 4

You need time and patience for making a risotto. It's like foreplay: you spend a lot of time at the pot, keeping it moist and when all the wet stuff cooks away, wet it again; the end result should be creamy and tender – well worth the time spent! So get your glass of wine … and stay with the heat.

10 ml (2 t) olive oil
250 g mushrooms, sliced
25 ml (5 t) butter
1 onion, peeled and finely chopped
2 cloves garlic, crushed
250 ml (1 c) uncooked risotto rice
handful of sundried tomatoes
1,25 litres (5 c) boiling chicken stock
125 ml (½ c) dry white wine
85 ml (⅓ c) grated Parmesan cheese
125 ml (½ c) roughly chopped Italian parsley

METHOD
1. Heat the olive oil in a large frying pan and fry the mushrooms. Remove from the pan.
2. In the same pan, heat the butter and fry the onion and garlic until transparent.
3. Add the risotto rice and sundried tomatoes and toss gently to coat in butter.
4. Add ⅓ each of the stock and wine, stirring constantly. Simmer until almost all the liquid has been absorbed.
5. Repeat until the stock and wine have all been used and the rice is tender. Cooking time should be 35–40 minutes.
6. Stir in the Parmesan cheese and the parsley, and serve.

* Keep the stock hot.

Big Pan Open Omelette
Serves 4

45 ml (3 T) olive oil
1 onion, peeled and thinly sliced
1 red sweet pepper, cored, seeded and thinly sliced
1 yellow sweet pepper, cored, seeded and thinly sliced
15 ml (1 T) butter
2 cloves garlic, crushed
1 baby marrow, trimmed and thinly sliced
salt and milled black pepper
150 g Cheddar cheese, grated
250 ml (1 c) cream
5 eggs, beaten
30 ml (2 T) grated Parmesan cheese (optional)

METHOD
1. Heat the oil in a frying pan and fry the onion and peppers over low heat until softened.
2. Add the butter, garlic and baby marrow, give a stir and season well.
3. Mix the Cheddar cheese and cream into the eggs, pour over vegetables and stir lightly to mix. Make sure the egg mixture covers the base of the pan.
4. Cook gently over a low heat until just set.
5. Sprinkle with Parmesan cheese, if using, and serve with tossed baby rocket, cos lettuce and Bella tomatoes.

Roasted Coriander Potatoes
Serves as many as you need

Great hot, and cold. If you cook them really crisp and put them in a big bowl to pass around, they are better than crisps.

300 g new potatoes, washed
2 cloves garlic, crushed
125 ml (½ c) fresh coriander
rock salt to taste
125 ml (½ c) olive oil
juice of 1 lemon
2 long stalks rosemary
black pepper to taste

SOUR CREAM DRESSING
1 clove garlic, crushed
250 ml (1 c) sour cream
125 ml (½ c) chopped chives
5 ml (1 t) grated lemon zest
salt and milled black pepper

METHOD
1. Preheat the oven to 200 °C.
2. Parboil the potatoes until half-cooked. Drain.
3. Cut in half lengthways. Toss in remaining ingredients, except the dressing.
4. Roast until crisp.
5. Mix all the dressing ingredients together.
6. Serve the potatoes hot, cold or lukewarm, with or without the dressing.

* I always prepare the potatoes and their coating the day before I am going to cook them so that the flavours have time to infuse.
* Roast the potatoes with the herbs and the juice to make them all sticky and crisp.

Crushed New Potatoes with Feta, Coriander, deep-fried Capers and Green Peppercorns

Serves 6

500 g new potatoes, steamed in their jackets
15 ml (1 T) green Madagascar peppercorns
30 ml (2 T) deep-fried capers
250 ml (1 c) sour cream
olive oil
3 rounds feta cheese, crumbled
125 ml (½ c) roughly chopped fresh coriander
salt and milled black pepper

METHOD
1. When potatoes are ready, crush (not mash) them.
2. Fling the rest of the ingredients into the potatoes. Mix through.
3. Serve with poached chicken or fish, on a pile of wilted spinach (English spinach is great).

* Always add capers towards the end of cooking, as lengthy cooking tends to bring out a bitter flavour.
* Try caper flowers, they are big, juicy and delicious.
* More sour cream never hurt anyone!

New Potatoes with a Yoghurt Dressing

Serves 6

You can serve this hot or cold, but for great oral satisfaction eat them while the skins are still hot and tight and burst as you bite them … try it!

10 medium new potatoes in their jackets, boiled till tender

DRESSING
juice and grated zest of 1 lemon
125 ml (½ c) fat-free natural yoghurt
125 ml (½ c) olive oil
125 ml (½ c) chopped Italian parsley
30 ml (2 T) chopped fresh dill
salt and milled black pepper
2 ml (½ t) castor sugar

METHOD
1. Blend all the dressing ingredients together.
2. Cut the potatoes into quarters and toss into dressing.

Sweet Potato and Parsnip Mash
Serves 6

I love to serve baked fish on top of this mash.

2 fat parsnips, peeled, sliced and steamed until tender
400 g red-skinned sweet potatoes, peeled and steamed until tender
75 ml (5 T) butter
150 ml (⅗ c) cream
5 ml (1 t) grated orange zest
1 clove garlic, crushed
splash of orange juice
salt and milled black pepper

TO SERVE
Gingered Carrots (see recipe on page 57)
6 baked fish slices
Roasted Rosa Tomatoes (see recipe on page 44)
blanched asparagus spears (optional)

METHOD
1. Mash the parsnips and sweet potato while hot.
2. Mix in the butter, cream, grated orange zest and garlic.
3. Add a splash of orange juice. Season with salt and black pepper.
4. Dish mash onto 6 plates, top with gingered carrots, then place the fish on top. Cover fish with roasted tomatoes and, if wanted, a few blanched asparagus spears. This will produce the trendy tower effect.

* This quantity of butter never seems to be enough for me; add more if you wish.
* Lightly steam some young parsnips, then roast them till crisp and serve with roast dinner.

Butter Bean and Coriander Mash
Serves 8

I suppose I'd better rave about the wonderful benefits of beans: I love them, I mean really love them. They are full of fibre, high in protein, vitamins and minerals… need I go on? Try this dish – it will blow you away!

500 g dried butter beans, soaked overnight and drained
125 ml (½ c) olive oil
1 onion, peeled and finely chopped
4 cloves garlic, crushed
250 ml (1 c) roughly chopped coriander
15 ml (1 T) chopped flat-leafed parsley
1 green chilli, finely sliced
juice of 1 large lemon
salt and milled black pepper
big knob of butter

METHOD
1. Place the drained beans in a large saucepan and cover to double their depth with cold water.
2. Bring to the boil, reduce heat and simmer, covered, until the beans are tender. Drain.
3. Heat the olive oil and fry the onion until soft. Add the garlic, herbs and beans and mash roughly.
4. Add the lemon juice and season with salt and pepper.
5. Add the butter and mix well.

* You can add more olive oil if you wish; I do.
* This is also fabulous with A Twist in the Oxtail (see recipe on page 108).
* 500 g dried beans cooks up to 1 kg.
* Never add salt to beans while they are cooking; this prevents softening.

Polenta Mash
Serves 6-8

My friend Bianca Coleman is crazy about this. This one is for you, Bianca.
It started with the scrapings of the polenta pot and what we had lying around the kitchen at my cooking school. I then turned it into a fully-fledged meal – I must admit I used indecent amounts of butter and garlic with the pot scrapings! You could also serve it with A Twist in the Oxtail (see recipe on page 108)

1 x 1 kg packet polenta
100 g butter
lots of crushed garlic
big handfuls of wild rocket
as much shaved Parmesan as you like
salt and milled black pepper to taste

METHOD
1. Make the polenta according to the instructions on the packet – it doesn't get easier than that!
2. Pour the cooked polenta into a roasting pan and let it cool.
3. When it is set, cut it up roughly. Put to one side.
4. Melt butter in a hot frying pan, add the garlic and polenta and fry.
5. Add the rocket and Parmesan and stir through. Put the pan on the table and eat!

Creamy Parmesan Rice with Wilted Greens, Whole Black Mushrooms and Roasted Tomatoes

Serves 4

CREAMY RICE
250 ml (1 c) cooked rice per person
500 ml (2 c) white sauce
1 clove garlic, crushed
chopped fresh basil to taste
100 g Parmesan cheese, grated
salt and milled black pepper
herbs of your choice (flat-leafed parsley goes well with basil)

SPINACH
300 g spinach, chopped
125 ml (½ c) cream
knob of butter
shake of grated nutmeg
salt and milled black pepper

MUSHROOMS AND TOMATOES
4 plum tomatoes, halved
olive oil for drizzling
2 cloves garlic, crushed
salt and milled black pepper
4 large black mushrooms

METHOD
1. Preheat the oven to 200 °C.
2. Add the rice to the white sauce with the garlic, basil and cheese. Season to taste.
3. Lightly steam the spinach and drain. Add the cream and butter and season.
4. Drizzle the tomatoes with a little olive oil, sprinkle with a little garlic and season.
5. Bake for 20 minutes, then remove.
6. Rub the mushrooms with oil and garlic.
7. Pan-fry for 4 minutes, turning once.
8. Remove from the pan and keep warm.
9. Divide the rice between 4 plates, reserving a spoonful from each to top mushrooms.
10. Place spinach, then a mushroom (upside down), on top of rice.
11. Place the reserved rice in each mushroom cap and top with tomatoes.
12. Sprinkle with freshly chopped herbs.

Fried Rice
Serves 4

Always plan more than one meal when cooking rice – it is so healthy and versatile and can really stretch a meal. Cook a little extra for the next day.
This is normally a Sunday night light meal for my family.

60 ml (4 T) peanut oil
2 chicken breast fillets, sliced thinly
6 spring onions, chopped
1 stalk celery, sliced
1 red sweet pepper, sliced
1 chilli, sliced
2 carrots, julienned
2 cloves garlic, crushed
5 ml (1 t) palm sugar (from specialised delis and some supermarkets)
30 ml (2 T) fish sauce
15 ml (1 T) soy sauce
750 ml (3 c) cooked long-grain rice
3 eggs, beaten
fresh coriander

METHOD
1. Heat the oil and stir-fry the chicken for 3 minutes. Remove from the pan.
2. Add all the vegetables and garlic to the pan and stir-fry for 5 minutes.
3. Add the palm sugar and mix well.
4. Add the fish sauce, soy sauce and rice. Mix well.
5. Remove from the heat and mix in the chicken.
6. Make an omelette with the eggs. When cooked, slice into strips and pull through the rice with your fingers.
7. Season with more soy sauce if needed.
8. Garnish with fresh coriander.

ec-stacy

4

SINFUL &

SENSUAL

MAINS

Food is about your senses; your eyes, your hands, your mouth and tongue. You need to get aroused by the taste of a moist pink slice of smoked salmon, or the silky feel as you run your fingers down the flesh of a roasted red sweet pepper; the sensation as you stroke the firm, pink flesh of a plump chicken breast. You need to fall in love with fresh.

Thai Chicken Cakes
Serves 4

```
500 g minced chicken breast
125 ml (½ c) chopped coriander
1 bunch spring onion, with tops, thinly sliced
2 cloves garlic, crushed
15 ml (1 T) red curry paste
15 ml (1 T) Taste of Thai seasoning
5 ml (1 t) brown sugar
5 ml (1 t) Taste of Thai fish sauce
375 ml (1½ c) thinly sliced green beans
oil for frying
1 bottle (250 ml) Glaze 'n Baste™ (your choice of Mild, Medium or Hot)
```

METHOD
1. Mix all the ingredients, except the oil and baste, together.
2. Heat the oil in a frying pan.
3. Place heaped teaspoons of the chicken mixture in the frying pan and brown. Turn over and press down to flatten, then fry until browned and cooked through.
4. Serve with Giggling Gourmet™ Glaze 'n Baste™ sauce. Use the Mild, Medium or Hot version, according to your preference.

ecstacy

Tarragon Chicken
Serves 4

I have been blessed with a wonderful family and wonderful friends, but I've not been blessed with time. This is a dish I fling together when I've got in late and have friends coming to dinner.

100 g butter
8 chicken breasts cut into chunks
250 g button mushrooms, sliced
15 ml (1 T) dried tarragon
2 cloves garlic, crushed
100 ml (⅔ c) old brown sherry
salt and milled black pepper
250 ml (1 c) cream
15 ml (1 T) good-quality whole-grain mustard

METHOD
1. Heat half the butter and gently fry the chicken breasts until just touched with colour. Remove from the pan.
2. Add the remaining butter and fry the mushrooms, tarragon and garlic.
3. Add the sherry and cook until it has almost evaporated.
4. Season with salt and pepper. Add the cream and boil, uncovered, over high heat until reduced by half. Return the chicken to the pan and cook until heated through. Stir in the mustard.
5. Serve with noodles and a huge salad of baby salad leaves.

Paprika Chicken
Serves 4

20 ml (4 t) olive oil
8 chicken thighs
25 g butter
2 onions, peeled and thinly sliced
2 ml (½ t) caraway seeds
5 ml lightly bashed fennel seeds
3 cloves garlic, crushed
15 ml (1 T) paprika
1 x 400 g can tomatoes
2 red sweet peppers, thickly sliced into rings
salt and milled black pepper
250 ml (1 c) sour cream
parsley – Italian of course – roughly chopped

METHOD
1. Heat the oil in a large saucepan and brown the chicken in batches. Remove from the pan.
2. Whack the butter into the pan and let it sizzle. Add the onions, caraway seeds, fennel and garlic. Cook until tender and golden.
3. Add the paprika, give it a stir, add the tomatoes and return the chicken to the saucepan. Add the peppers and simmer for 35 minutes. Don't forget to season.
4. Pour in the sour cream, sprinkle with parsley and serve.

How to eat it:
On crushed boiled potatoes, with fresh parsley over the top.

* "Roughly chopped" means "Don't chop so hard that you leave the juices on the chopping board".
* Caraway seeds are used in rye bread, and are wonderful with pork, duck and apples. Try them with tomatoes too.

Peanut Chicken
Serves 4

30 ml (2 T) peanut oil
2 red chillies, sliced
1 bunch spring onions, roughly chopped
3 cloves garlic, crushed
500 g chicken breast fillets, cut into strips
5 ml (1 t) brown sugar
250 ml (1 c) sliced button mushrooms
salt and milled black pepper
1 x 400 g can coconut cream
fresh coriander
250 ml (1 c) salted peanuts, toasted

METHOD
1. Heat a large frying pan and add the peanut oil.
2. Add the chilli, spring onions and garlic. Keep the mixture moving in the pan for 2 minutes, then whack in the chicken, brown sugar and mushrooms.
3. Season with salt and pepper, and add coconut cream.
4. Turn up the heat and cook the sauce, uncovered, over high heat until it is reduced sufficiently to coat the chicken.
5. Fling in the coriander and switch off the stove. Spoon onto sticky rice and eat, topped with peanuts.

* "Keep it moving" means to stir to avoid burning.

How to buy garlic
Always choose firm heads without mould or sprouting.

* Garlic is good for lowering blood pressure and cholesterol levels.

Coriander Chicken
Serves 4

A good bachelor's dish. Don't overcook the chicken; every mouthful of chicken breast should be succulent, moist and tender.

olive oil
4 chicken breasts, cut into chunks
6 spring onions, roughly chopped
3 cloves garlic, crushed
1 red sweet pepper, sliced
Glaze 'n Baste™
a handful of fresh coriander
salt and milled black pepper

1. Heat the olive oil in a heavy-based pan.
2. Add the chicken, spring onions and garlic and stir-fry for 5 minutes.
3. Add the red pepper and Glaze 'n Baste, and fry lightly for 3 minutes.
4. Add the coriander and serve with couscous.
5. Season with salt & black pepper to taste.

How to eat it:
Sprinkle some sesame oil over, and toss a good handful of toasted nuts like cashews, pecans, or pine nuts over.

Parmesan Chicken
Serves 8

The longer the chicken stays in the sauce before serving, the better it will taste. Great with ciabatta and roasted tomatoes.

1 bay leaf
1 onion, peeled and thickly sliced
10 peppercorns
3 sprigs of thyme
1 stalk celery, chopped
1 litre (4 c) water
6 chicken breast fillets

SAUCE
250 ml (1 c) really good mayonnaise
250 ml (1 c) shredded fresh basil
1 clove garlic, crushed
125 ml (½ c) chopped sundried tomatoes
juice of 1 lemon
salt and milled black pepper
250 ml (1 c) shaved Parmesan cheese
30 ml (2 T) toasted pine nuts

METHOD
1. Combine the bay leaf, onion, peppercorns, thyme, celery and water in a saucepan and boil, uncovered, until the liquid is reduced by half. Strain.
2. Pour into a clean saucepan and bring to a rolling boil. Add the chicken breasts.
3. Close with the lid and bring back to the boil. Switch off the stove and let the chicken stand in the hot liquid for about 40 minutes. Don't lift the lid.
4. Remove the chicken and slice neatly. Reheat the stock and pour a few spoonfuls onto the chicken slices.
5. Now make sauce. Gently mix everything together, except the pine nuts.
6. Add the chicken and toss to coat. Top with pine nuts and serve on a bed of rocket.

Black Bean Chilli Chicken
Serves 4

You have to use all the chillies in this dish; the warm sensation it leaves in your mouth is just wonderful. But I have to warn you that oral sex will probably be out of the question for some time.

1 kg chicken breast fillets
30 ml (2 T) oil
1 large onion, peeled and roughly chopped
4 cloves garlic, roughly chopped
4 red chillies, julienned
100 ml (⅖ c) black bean sauce (from delis and some supermarkets)
200 g baby green beans, roughly chopped
soy sauce to taste
splash of sesame oil

METHOD
1. Cut the chicken into strips.
2. Heat the oil in a large saucepan, add the onion and fry gently until translucent.
3. Add the chicken, garlic and chilli and stir-fry for 5 minutes.
4. Add the black bean sauce and green beans and cook for 10 minutes.
5. Season to taste with soy sauce, drizzle with sesame oil and serve with rice or noodles.

Orange Chilli Chicken
Serves 4

Using red chillies will add colour and bite.

4 chicken breast fillets, chopped
30 ml (2 T) peanut oil
2 chillies, sliced
3 cloves garlic, crushed
2 oranges, peeled and cut into segments
1 bunch chopped spring onions
1 x 400 g can coconut cream
250 ml (1 c) chopped fresh basil
125 ml (½ c) fresh coriander

METHOD
1. Slice each chicken breast into 5 pieces.
2. Heat the peanut oil and gently cook the chicken pieces with chilli and garlic for 7 minutes.
3. Add the orange segments and spring onions and cook for another 2 minutes.
4. Remove the chicken and oranges and stir the coconut cream into the pan.
5. Simmer for 10 minutes, then add the chicken, oranges, basil and coriander.
6. Heat through and serve with steamed jasmine rice and wilted spinach.

Peanut Chicken Bake
Serves 6

One of my most wonderful memories of Thailand was a small market in Chang Mai, where the locals went to buy their fresh-pressed coconut cream or milk. There were mounds of creamy fudgy palm sugar, which we just had to buy to bring home. Needless to say, it never ever got here … you can't imagine how it tasted, like gooey coconut fudge!

6 chicken breasts fillets

SAUCE
2 cloves garlic, crushed
125 ml (½ c) peanut butter
30 ml (2 T) tomato paste
30 ml (2 T) brown sugar or palm sugar
375 ml (1½ c) low-fat natural yoghurt
125 ml (½ c) chopped dhania
125 ml (½ c) torn basil
1 red chilli, sliced
5 ml (1 t) fish sauce

METHOD
1. Mix all the sauce ingredients together.
2. Add the chicken breasts, turn to coat and marinate for 3 hours.
3. Preheat the oven to 180 °C.
4. Place the chicken and sauce in an ovenproof dish and bake, covered, for 30 minutes.

* Palm sugar comes from the date, coconut, toddy and palmyra palms. The sap is collected by tapping either the trunk or the top of the tree.

Soviet Chicken
Serves 4

4 chicken breast fillets
salt and milled black pepper to taste
45 ml (3 T) grated lemon zest
1 clove garlic, crushed
125 ml (½ c) fresh breadcrumbs
15 ml (1 T) chopped fresh dill
500 ml (2 c) sour cream

60 ml (4 T) salmon trout roe
30 ml (2 T) butter
60 g Beluga caviar

METHOD
1. Make a pocket in the flesh of each chicken breast, and season inside and out with salt and black pepper.
2. Mix together the lemon zest, garlic, breadcrumbs and dill, and moisten with 125 ml (½ c) of the sour cream.
3. Stuff the chicken breasts with the breadcrumb mixture.
4. Place 15 ml (1 T) salmon roe on the stuffing in each chicken breast. Secure with toothpicks and chill until needed.
5. Preheat the oven to 180 °C.
6. Fry the chicken breasts in butter for 3 minutes on each side, then bake for 12 minutes.
7. Make the sauce. Mix together the caviar and remaining sour cream and spoon over the chicken.
8. Use some extra dill for garnishing.

Soy Chicken Stir-fry
Serves 6

1 kg chicken breast fillets, cut into strips
15 ml (1 T) olive oil
6 spring onions, chopped
2 cloves garlic, crushed
small piece fresh ginger, chopped
1 red sweet pepper, sliced
1 red chilli, sliced (optional)

MARINADE
10 ml (2 t) old brown sherry
5 ml (1 t) sesame oil
30 ml (2 T) sweet soy sauce
5 ml (1 t) fish sauce
2-5 ml (½-1 t) white pepper

METHOD
1. Mix the marinade ingredients together and marinate the chicken in it for 30 minutes.
2. Heat the oil in a frying pan and stir-fry the spring onions, garlic, ginger, sweet pepper and chilli for 5 minutes.
3. Add the chicken and stir-fry until the chicken is cooked through. Serve on sticky rice.

Thai Chicken Salad with Lime
Serves 4

On my travels in Thailand I fell in love with this lime dressing, which I use on fish, salads, roughly grated green pawpaw or green mangoes. Use it with Red Onion, Mango and Rocket Salad (see recipe on page 44). You need to use fresh limes, otherwise the recipe will not work.

1 punnet baby corn, roughly chopped
½ bunch spring onions, roughly chopped
handful mangetout, lightly blanched
handful baby beans, lightly blanched
2 carrots, julienned
250 ml (1 c) cauliflower florets
2 chicken breast fillets, lightly steamed and shredded
250 ml (1 c) unsalted peanuts, toasted
coriander, to garnish

LIME DRESSING
4 cloves garlic
4 red chillies
30 ml (2 T) palm sugar (from delis)
37 ml (2½ T) fish sauce
juice of 3 fresh limes
5 ml (1 t) grated lime zest

METHOD
1. First make the dressing. Pound together garlic and chillies in a mortar and pestle.
2. Add the palm sugar and fish sauce and pound to a paste.
3. Add the lime juice and zest and mix.
4. Taste and adjust the quantities of lime, palm sugar and fish sauce to suit your palate.
5. Marinate the vegetables for 2 hours in the dressing. Pull the chicken through just before serving.
6. Top with peanuts, garnish with fresh coriander and serve.

ecstacy

Sundried Tomato-stuffed Chicken Breasts
Serves 4

60 ml (4 T) ricotta
20 ml (4 t) sundried tomato pesto
2 cloves garlic, crushed
salt and milled black pepper
4 chicken breast fillets
4 baby spinach leaves
4 quarters of roasted red sweet peppers (see recipe on page 49)
olive oil

METHOD
1. Preheat the oven to 180 °C.
2. Mix together the ricotta, pesto and garlic and season to taste.
3. Place the chicken breasts on a chopping board and, using a sharp knife, cut a slit horizontally into the side of the breast to make a deep pocket, but don't cut all the way through.
4. Layer a spinach leaf and roasted pepper quarter in each pocket. Fill with stuffing, but do not over-fill. Secure with toothpicks.
5. Heat a little olive oil in a frying pan and fry the breasts gently on all sides to seal and colour them.
6. Bake for about 15 minutes.
7. Slice chicken and serve with creamy Polenta Mash (see recipe on page 74).

*   Use the largest of the baby spinach leaves to cover the inside of the chicken breast pockets.
*   Chicken breasts are never the same size – one is always a little bigger than the other – but do try to get them all about the same size to facilitate even cooking.

Chicken with Olives and Preserved Lemons
Serves 6

5 ml (1 t) ground ginger
2 ml (½ t) ground cumin
2 ml (½ t) paprika
pinch of saffron
2 ml (½ t) milled white pepper
6 chicken breast fillets, cubed
30 ml (2 T) olive oil
22 ml (1½ T) butter
2 onions, peeled and roughly chopped
2 cloves garlic, crushed
1 stick cinnamon
juice of ½ lemon
peel of 1 whole preserved lemon
315 ml (1¼ c) pitted black olives
125 ml (½ c) chopped flat-leaf parsley
125 ml (½ c) chopped coriander

METHOD
1. Mix the spices together and rub over the chicken.
2. Heat the oil and butter in a large frying pan.
3. Fry the onions and garlic, then add the chicken and cinnamon stick.
4. Add the lemon juice, preserved lemon and olives.
5. Cook for 10–15 minutes.
6. Stir in the parsley and coriander and serve with couscous.

Turkey loaf
Serves 6

800 g turkey mince
125 ml (½ c) chopped Italian parsley
100 g fresh white breadcrumbs
6 whole spring onions, chopped
4 eggs, beaten
5 ml (1 t) green peppercorns
125 ml (½ c) chopped red sweet peppers
250 ml (1 c) sliced button mushrooms
125 ml (½ c) sliced black olives
2 cloves garlic, crushed
5 ml (1 t) grated lemon zest
salt to taste

SAUCE
500 ml (2 c) low-fat natural yoghurt
1 clove garlic, crushed
juice of 1 lemon
125 ml (½ c) freshly chopped coriander
salt and milled black pepper

METHOD
1. Preheat the oven to 180 °C. Grease a 1 kg loaf pan.
2. Mix all the loaf ingredients together.
3. Spoon the mixture into the loaf pan, cover with foil and bake for 1 hour.
4. Remove from the oven and allow to stand in the pan for 30 minutes. Turn out and cool.
5. Mix the sauce ingredients together.
6. Slice the turkey loaf and serve with the herb and yoghurt sauce.

* Chicken mince can also be used.

Chicken Rice Balls
Serves 6

3 rounds feta cheese, crumbled
6 chicken breast fillets, minced
375 ml (1½ c) cooked long-grained rice
1 egg, beaten
6 spring onions, chopped
125 ml (½ c) chopped coriander
3 cloves garlic, crushed
250 ml (1 c) chopped mixed sweet peppers
salt and milled black pepper
olive oil

TOMATO SAUCE
olive oil
1 onion, peeled and diced
2 cloves garlic, crushed
1 x 400 g can chopped tomatoes
250 ml (1 c) sundried tomatoes
2 ml (½ t) chilli powder
5 ml (1 t) sugar
250 ml (1 c) fresh basil leaves

METHOD
1. Mix the feta, chicken, rice, egg, onions, coriander, garlic, sweet peppers and sea-soning together.
2. Fry small spoonfuls of the chicken mixture in heated olive oil until lightly browned. Set aside.
3. Make the tomato sauce. In the same frying pan, heat a little more oil and fry the onion and garlic until transparent.
4. Add the tomatoes, sundried tomatoes, chilli powder and sugar and simmer for 10 minutes.
5. Add the chicken balls and heat through. Stir in the basil.
6. Serve on a ring of rice.

Stuffed Beef Rolls
Serves 6

12 thin slices of rump (about 100 g each)
olive oil
250 ml (1 c) chicken stock
250 ml (1 c) white wine or verjuice (see Glossary)

STUFFING
100 g streaky bacon, chopped
30 ml (2 T) chopped capers
6 anchovy fillets, chopped
60 ml (4 T) roughly chopped Italian parsley
2 cloves garlic, crushed
milled black pepper
4 roasted red sweet peppers, sliced

METHOD
1. Mix all the stuffing ingredients together.
2. Spread out the slices of steak and top each one with stuffing.
3. Roll up each piece of steak and tie with string or cotton.
4. Heat a little olive oil in a frying pan and brown the beef rolls all over.
5. Turn the heat right down, then add the stock and wine to the pan.
6. Cover and simmer gently for 45 minutes.
7. Serve on Polenta Mash (see recipe on page 74) with a cos salad or steamed greens.

Beef Strips with Sundried Tomatoes and Red Sweet Peppers
Serves 6

75 ml (5 T) olive oil
1 kg beef strips
2 medium onions, peeled and thinly sliced
4 large sweet red peppers, quartered and roasted
10 ml (2 t) dried oregano
3 fat cloves garlic, crushed
250 ml (1 c) sundried tomatoes
10 ml (2 t) tomato purée
pinch of sugar
salt and milled black pepper to taste

METHOD
1. Heat the oil in a large saucepan.
2. Stir-fry beef, in batches, until browned. Remove from the pan and set aside.
3. Fry the onions, sweet peppers, oregano and garlic, sundried tomatoes and toma-to purée for about 5 minutes.
4. Add a pinch of sugar and salt and pepper to taste.
5. Return the beef to the pan, heat through and serve.

Baked Lamb and Brinjal Wraps smothered in a Parmesan Cheese Sauce

Serves 6

18 large brinjal slices
olive oil
2 onions, peeled and finely chopped
3 cloves garlic, crushed
500 g lamb mince
100 ml (½ glass) red wine – drink the rest!
15 ml (1 T) chopped fresh rosemary
4 fresh tomatoes, chopped
salt and milled black pepper
15 ml (1 T) tomato purée
pinch of sugar
250 ml (1 c) fresh breadcrumbs
white sauce (see recipe on page 157)
125 ml (½ T) roughly chopped Italian parsley
125 ml (½ c) freshly grated Parmesan cheese

METHOD

1. Lightly salt the brinjal slices and set aside for 30 minutes. Rinse, drain and pat dry.
2. Heat a little oil in a frying pan and fry brinjal slices on both sides. Set aside on absorbent paper to drain.
3. Heat a little oil in a large saucepan and gently fry the onions and garlic.
4. Add the lamb mince and stir-fry until it is no longer pink.
5. Add the wine, rosemary and tomatoes, black pepper and purée. Simmer gently, until the sauce is reduced and thickened, then add the sugar and salt.
6. Mix in the breadcrumbs. Place spoonfuls of the mixture on the brinjal slices, then roll them up. Arrange in an ovenproof dish. Preheat the oven to 180 °C.
7. Make the white sauce and stir in the parsley and Parmesan cheese.
8. Whack it all over the brinjal rolls and bake until golden.
9. Garnish with shaved Parmesan cheese and milled black pepper. Drizzle with olive oil and serve.

How to buy brinjals

Choose brinjals that have long necks, like a swan. The fruit should be bright purple in colour, firm and with a well-rounded bottom. Weigh them up in your hands: the feel should tell you whether they are spongy, or hard and firm.

Lamb Shanks roasted in paper
Serves 6

This dish is great for showing off your sucking skills – don't leave a drop of marrow behind! Make the dish for two, and freeze the leftovers.

6 meaty lamb shanks

MARINADE
90 ml (6 T) olive oil
4 cloves garlic, crushed
5 ml (1 t) paprika
250 ml (1 c) lemon juice
1 onion, peeled and finely chopped
20 black peppercorns
fresh rosemary, thyme and parsley, chopped

METHOD
1. Mix all the marinade ingredients together and marinate the lamb shanks for 24 hours.
2. Remove the lamb from marinade. Pat dry.
3. Preheat the oven to 160 °C.
4. Place each shank on 2 layers of buttered greaseproof paper or aluminium foil.
5. Season with salt and top with herbs.
6. Wrap up tightly, tucking the ends under so they won't open during cooking.
7. Place the parcels in a well-greased baking dish.
8. Bake the shanks for 3 hours. Don't add liquid and don't turn.
9. Serve on creamy, Butter Bean and Coriander Mash (see recipe on page 73) and honey-glazed Gingered Carrots (see recipe on page 57).

Stuffed Leg of Lamb
Serves 6-8

When I use garlic, they have to be obese cloves, the fattest I can find. I don't mean elephant garlic, with its mild, sweet creamy flavour – that's for roasting and spreading onto crisp grilled ciabatta.

1,75 kg boned leg of lamb
salt and milled black pepper
250 ml (1 c) rosemary needles

STUFFING
olive oil
3 spring onions, finely chopped
6 button mushrooms, finely chopped
50 g stale breadcrumbs
15 ml (1 T) chopped Italian parsley
15 ml (1 T) pine nuts
5 ml (1 t) grated lemon zest
3 cloves garlic, crushed
50 g haloumi cheese, grated
30 ml (2 T) lemon juice
salt and milled black pepper

METHOD
1. First make the stuffing. Heat a little olive oil in a frying pan and gently fry the spring onions and mushrooms.
2. Remove from the heat.
3. Place the breadcrumbs, parsley, pine nuts, lemon zest, garlic, haloumi cheese, lemon juice, salt and pepper in a bowl.
4. Add the mushrooms and spring onions and mix well.
5. Open the lamb out flat, and spread the stuffing all over it. Roll it up and tie with string.
6. Rub a little olive oil onto the meat and season well with salt and pepper.
7. Preheat the oven to 180 °C.
8. Place the rosemary needles in the base of a roasting pan.
9. Pop the lamb on top and roast for 1 hour, or a little longer for well done.
10. Remove from the oven and allow to stand in a warm place for 10-15 minutes to rest before carving. This makes carving easier and retains the juices and flavour.

ecstacy

Fillets in Yoghurt Sauce
Serves 6

30 ml (2 T) butter or olive oil
750 g beef fillet, cut into strips
1 onion, peeled and chopped
500 ml (2 c) sliced button mushrooms
5 ml (1 t) dried basil
1 clove garlic, crushed
125 ml (½ c) dry white wine or sweet sherry
salt to taste
250 ml (1 c) sour cream or low-fat natural yoghurt
2 ml (½ t) green peppercorns
10 ml (2 t) Dijon mustard

METHOD
1. Heat the butter or oil in a frying pan and fry the meat in batches to seal on all sides. Remove and set aside. Don't overcook.
2. Add the onion to the pan and cook until translucent, then add the mushrooms, basil and garlic. Stir-fry for 5 minutes, add the wine and cook over high heat, uncovered, until the sauce is reduced by half.
3. Return the meat to the pan, with any juices, and heat through.
4. Season with salt. Add cream or yoghurt, peppercorns and mustard. Stir through, then remove from the stove and serve with noodles.

* Chicken fillets can also be used.

A Twist in the Oxtail
Serves 8

Bite the tips of the bones and suck out all that delicious marrow.

2 oxtails, cut up
enough flour for dusting
salt and milled black pepper
30 ml (2 T) olive oil
50 ml (⅕ c) butter
4 cloves garlic, crushed
2 large onions, peeled and chopped
30 ml (2 T) harissa paste
1 x 400 g can tomatoes
30 ml (2 T) tomato purée
500 ml (2 c) red wine
1 x 425 g can butter beans, drained
1 x 425 g can chickpeas, drained

GREMOLATA
15 ml (1 T) finely grated lemon zest
2 cloves garlic, finely chopped
125 ml (½ c) finely chopped parsley
1 red chilli, finely chopped

METHOD
1. Dust the oxtail with seasoned flour.
2. Heat the oil and butter in a large saucepan and brown the oxtail in small batches.
3. Remove and set aside.
4. Add the garlic and onion to the saucepan and cook until soft but not brown.
5. Stir in the harissa paste and cook for 5 minutes.
6. Stir in the tomatoes, tomato purée and red wine and return the oxtail to the saucepan.
7. Simmer gently until the oxtail is tender, then add the beans and chickpeas and simmer for a further 15 minutes.
8. Mix all the ingredients for the gremolata.
9. Serve the beef on Polenta Mash (see recipe on page 74) and top with gremolata.

ecstacy

Baked Yellowtail
Serves 4

Always cook yellowtail on the day of purchase and never overcook it!

4 x 250 g yellowtail steaks or fillets
salt and milled black pepper
olive oil
lemon juice
butter
6 cloves of garlic, crushed
fresh rosemary needles

METHOD
1. Preheat the oven to 180 °C.
2. Season the fish with salt and black pepper.
3. Heat a little olive oil in a heavy-based frying pan and seal the fish quickly on both sides.
4. Transfer the fish to a baking sheet, and squeeze lemon juice over the steaks or fillets.
5. Top each with a blob of butter and crushed garlic, and sprinkle rosemary needles over.
6. Bake for about 8–10 minutes, then remove from the oven and set aside.

Prawn and Fish Cakes
Serves 4-6

Coconut cream freezes well, so decant the rest of the can into a freezer container and freeze until you need it for the next curry you make.

5 ml (1 t) fish sauce
5 ml (1 t) red curry paste
5 ml (1 t) palm sugar or brown sugar
100 ml (⅖ c) coconut cream
200 g prawn meat, chopped
500 g kingklip, finely diced
1 bunch spring onions, sliced - tops and all
2 garlic cloves, crushed
250 ml (1 c) roughly chopped coriander
125 ml (½ c) roughly chopped fresh basil
olive oil for frying

METHOD
1. Mix the fish sauce, curry paste, palm sugar and coconut cream together until smooth.
2. Add to the remaining ingredients, except the oil, in a bowl and mix well.
3. Shape into fish cakes and refrigerate until firm, at least 1 hour.
4. Heat the oil and shallow-fry the fish cakes on both sides until golden.
5. Serve hot with Lime Dressing (see recipe on page 92).

Roasted Kingklip with Lemon Coriander Sauce

Serves 4

juice of 1 lemon
4 thick slices of kingklip, each weighing 250 g
salt and milled black pepper
paprika
olive oil

SAUCE
125 ml (½ c) cream
75 ml (5 T) butter
½ medium bunch coriander, chopped
30 ml (2 T) lemon juice

METHOD

1. Squeeze lemon juice over the kingklip and season with salt, pepper and paprika. Let this rest for 20 minutes. Meanwhile, preheat the oven to 180 °C.
2. Heat the olive oil in a frying pan.
3. Sear fish on both sides, but don't cook through. Remove from the heat.
4. Place on a baking sheet and roast for 8–10 minutes.
5. Remove and keep warm while making the sauce.
6. Heat the cream with half the butter and the coriander.
7. Simmer for 4–5 minutes, or until slightly reduced.
8. Add the lemon juice, stir for 1 minute, then remove from the heat.
9. Whisk In the remaining butter, a few pieces at a time. Check seasoning. Serve over fish.

* Serve this sauce with steamed asparagus and Gingered Carrots (See recipe on page 57).
* Green beans and potato wedges make good accompaniments.

Grilled Swordfish
Serves 4

We are seeing a lot more of swordfish these days – you must try some!

My memories of a little Greek town – wooden trestles covered with white paper, bowls of chunky Greek salad, glistening lemon wedges, thick slices of bread, swollen black olives and olive oil – come to life when I make this dish.

```
1 thick swordfish or tuna steak, weighing 1 kg
butter for blobbing

MARINADE
125 ml (½ c) chopped fresh thyme
juice of 2 lemons
125 ml (½ c) olive oil
4 cloves garlic, chopped
salt and milled black pepper
```

METHOD
1. Cut the swordfish into 4 steaks.
2. Whisk the marinade ingredients together.
3. Pour the marinade over the fish and marinate in the fridge for 1 hour, turning once after 30 minutes.
4. Heat a lightly oiled grilling pan until it is hell-hot.
5. Pan-grill swordfish until it is almost done.
6. Place each steak on a plate.
7. Blob with butter and serve with the chunky salad etc.

* Always buy swordfish with a clean, well-defined bloodline.
* Don't overcook the fish, as it continues to cook when removed from the heat source. It's always better when it is succulent and moist.
* You could also heat the marinade, remove it from the heat and whisk in little knobs of butter until it tastes the way you like it; I do!

Seared Tuna on a bed of wilted Oriental Spinach (Tah Tsai)
Serves 4

Tah tsai sounds like a swear word but it is a marvellous oriental vegetable. Most supermarkets now stock oriental vegetables, but if you cannot find the spinach, use English spinach instead.

1 lemon
4 x 200 g tuna steaks, seared on both sides
salt and milled black pepper
olive oil
20 ml (4 t) Glaze 'n Baste™ (Medium)
sesame oil for drizzling

WILTED TAH TSAI
1 head tah tsai per person, root trimmed
15 ml (1 T) olive oil
soy sauce

METHOD
1. Squeeze the lemon juice over the tuna and season the fish with salt and pepper.
2. Heat the oil until very hot, then very quickly sear the tuna on both sides.
3. Remove from the pan, top each slice with 5 ml (1 t) Glaze 'n Baste, and serve on wilted tah tsai.
4. Drizzle a little sesame oil over if you like; I do!
5. Heat the oil, add the tah tsai and stir-fry fast until wilted. Splash with soy sauce, remove from heat and serve with tuna.

* Cook the tah tsai quickly to keep it crisp.
* Whatever you do, don't over-cook the tuna; medium-rare and no more.

Marinated Tuna with fresh Herbs, Capers and Peppers
Serves 5-6

I am so tuned in to tuna … I'm talking fresh tuna; this dish can only be made with very, very fresh tuna. This reminds me of Mauritius, but we won't talk about that now!

500 g fresh tuna, trimmed of all dark meat

MARINADE
125 ml (½ c) capers
15 ml (1 T) green peppercorns
125 ml (½ c) freshly chopped Italian parsley
125 ml (½ c) torn fresh basil
1 red onion, peeled and thinly sliced
60 ml (4 T) extra-virgin olive oil
30 ml (2 T) lemon or lime juice
salt and milled black pepper

PEPPER SALAD
5 roasted mixed peppers (see recipe on page 49)
olive oil
1 clove garlic, crushed
salt flakes

METHOD
1. Cut the tuna into slices about 10 mm thick, then cut each slice into strips.
2. Mix all the marinade ingredients together.
3. Toss the tuna into the marinade, turning gently with your hands to coat each and every piece.
4. Refrigerate for 2 hours, turning after 1 hour.
5. Make the salad. Cut roasted peppers into strips.
6. Mix with a little olive oil, crushed garlic and flaked salt.
7. Serve the tuna with grilled ciabatta topped with the pepper salad and enjoy.

* Serve as a starter, platter for buffet or hand around at a braai.
* Garnish with Maldon salt flakes; the flavour is clean and chemical-free.

Baked Cob on a bed of Sliced Fennel
Serves 6

You can leave the head on if you like, but cover the eye when you bring it to the table. Don't throw the fennel tops away; you will need them.

1 x 1,5-2 kg whole cob, butterflied, head off, skin on
100 ml (½ glass) dry white wine
salt and milled black pepper
2 cloves garlic, crushed
100 g cold butter, sliced
3 whole, big-bottomed fennel bulbs
olive oil for coating the fennel

METHOD
1. Preheat the oven to 220 °C.
2. Open the fish out flat. Pour over the wine, season with salt and pepper and rub in the crushed garlic.
3. Top with sliced butter and some of the fennel tops. Set aside.
4. Slice the fennel bulbs quite thickly.
5. Toss in olive oil, season with salt and pepper and place in the bottom of an oven pan.
6. Place the fish on the fennel.
7. Rub the skin of the fish with a little olive oil and bake for 20–25 minutes.
8. Serve with a mound of spring onion mash* and steamed baby beans.

* To make spring onion mash, chop 6 spring onions, including tops, sweat in a little butter and stir into mashed potato.

How to buy fish
The head should always be on, and the eyes should be bright, full and colourful – not jet-lagged. The gills should be red and fresh, and the scales moist and loose. Above all, the flesh should be firm; there shouldn't be anything dry or flabby about it at all. And, of course, it should not smell like fish, but only of the sea.

Baked Sardines with Thyme and Roasted Lemons

Serves 4

The smell of the sea hits you as you open the car door… you look out over the beach and it is heaving with people, the sea is boiling: it's the sardine run in Durban, with buckets, basins, skirts and shirts, every scoop a hit.

Grilled, baked or pan-fried, these seemingly forgotten little fish are delicious. Try them, I dare you!

2 whole heads of garlic
lots of olive oil
8 sardines, cleaned and heads left on
24 whole peppercorns
handful of fresh thyme
2 whole lemons
coarse salt
2 whole red chillies
250 ml (1 c) black olives

METHOD
1. Preheat the oven to 180 °C.
2. Halve the heads of garlic crossways. Drizzle with olive oil, place in a large shallow dish and bake for 25 minutes. Remove from the oven. Increase the heat to 200 °C.
3. Thread a wooden skewer through the mouth of each sardine.
4. Pack into the same dish as the garlic.
5. Add the peppercorns and strew with fresh thyme.
6. Cut the lemons in half and squeeze the juice all over the sardines, then place the lemons, cut side down, in the dish.
7. Salt the sardines and add the chillies and olives.
8. Drizzle with lots of olive oil and bake for 10 minutes.
9. Serve with a green salad and lots of crusty bread to mop up the juices.

* You can also add a cup of cherry tomatoes before baking the fish.
* Soak the skewers in hot water for 30 minutes before use. This will prevent their burning during cooking.
* Olive oil seduces the taste buds. Mop it all up!

ecstacy

Wok-cooked fragrant Mussels
Serves 6

2 kg mussels, well-scrubbed
olive oil
2 chillies
salt and milled black pepper
5 spring onions
2 cloves garlic
2 handfuls freshly chopped coriander
45 ml (3 T) fresh root ginger
15 ml (1 T) sesame oil
3 sticks lemon grass
3 limes
1 X 400 g can coconut milk

METHOD
1. Place mussels and a couple of lugs of olive oil in a large, very hot wok or saucepan.
2. Shake around, then add the rest of the ingredients, except the lime juice and coconut milk.
3. Keep turning the ingredients until all the mussels have opened up; throw away any that remain closed. Remove mussels and set aside.
4. Halve the limes and squeeze in the juice, then add coconut milk.
5. Bring to the boil. Remove from the heat and add the mussels.
6. Serve immediately as is.

Pickled Fish
Serves 6-8

2 kg firm white fish fillets
salt and milled black pepper
40 ml (8 t) cake flour
oil

CURRY SAUCE
750 ml (3 c) vinegar
250 ml (1 c) water
250 ml (1 c) sugar
15 ml (1 T) turmeric
30 ml (2 T) curry powder
5 ml (1 t) salt and 15 ml (1 T) black peppercorns
4 onions, peeled and sliced
6 lemon leaves
15 ml (1 T) crushed ginger
2 bay leaves
250 ml (1 c) sultanas

METHOD
1. Cut the fish into pieces and season. Dust with flour.
2. Heat oil in a large frying pan and fry the fish on both sides until cooked through. Drain on paper towels.
3. Make the curry sauce. Combine the vinegar, water, sugar, turmeric, curry powder, salt and peppercorns in a large saucepan. Bring to the boil.
4. Add the onions, lemon leaves, crushed ginger and bay leaves. Simmer for approximately 10 minutes. Do not overcook the onions; keep them crunchy!
5. Mix 15 ml (1 T) flour into a little of the sauce. Stir over high heat until it thickens.
6. Fling in the sultanas and stir well.
7. Layer the fish and onions in a glass dish. Pour the sauce over. Cover, cool and then refrigerate.
8. Let the fish stand for 3 days before eating.

* It's only OK to lick the spoon if it's not going back into the dish; otherwise you are going contaminate the contents. Always use a clean spoon when dishing up.
* Pickled fish will keep for up to 1 month, stored airtight in a clean glass container, in the fridge.

Haddock and Macaroni Brunch Bake
Serves 6 or 4 starving adults

May your yolk ooze all over your spinach.

250 ml (1 c) roughly chopped flat-leafed parsley
500 ml (2 c) cooked macaroni
salt and milled black pepper
500 ml (2 c) cooked spinach
600 ml (2⅖ c) Cheese Sauce (make double quantity of the recipe on
  page 157)
500 g haddock, poached and flaked
6 eggs
1 large onion, peeled and sliced into thin rings

METHOD
1. Preheat the oven to 180 °C.
2. Mix together the parsley and macaroni.
3. Season with salt and milled black pepper and spread out over the bottom of an ovenproof dish.
4. Top with spinach and cover with half the cheese sauce.
5. Add the flaked haddock, break the eggs on top and pour the remaining cheese sauce over. Top with sliced onions.
6. Bake until the eggs are set and yolks are still runny; about 20 minutes, depending on your oven.
7. Serve with hot crusty bread and lashings of butter, and a large bowl of tossed rocket dressed with lemon juice and olive oil.

* A good strong Cheddar cheese works well in this recipe; use it in the sauce.

Fish Pie
Serves 6

100 g butter
800 g large raw prawns, cleaned and deveined
400 g kingklip, cut into large chunks
salt and milled black pepper
2 cloves garlic, crushed
10 ml (2 t) grated lemon zest
splash of lemon juice
1 bunch spring onions, chopped
30 g flour
5 ml (1 t) dried dill or 15 ml (1 T) chopped fresh dill
250 ml (1 c) fish stock
150 ml (⅗ c) dry white wine
250 ml (1 c) cream

RICE TOPPING
500 ml (2 c) cooked rice
10 ml (2 t) grated lemon rind
30 ml (2 T) chopped chives
big knob of butter
1 clove garlic, crushed
2 eggs, beaten
250 ml (1 c) cream
salt and milled black pepper

ecstacy

METHOD

1. Heat half the butter in a large saucepan and fry prawns gently until just pink (don't overcook). Remove from the saucepan.
2. Season the kingklip with a little salt and pepper, then add to the saucepan with the garlic and lemon zest and fry gently on both sides until lightly golden. Add a splash of lemon juice and remove from the pan.
3. Add the spring onions to the pan with the remaining butter, the flour and dill, then stir and cook gently until wilted.
4. Add the stock and wine and cook, uncovered, over high heat until smooth and reduced by half.
5. Pour in the cream and cook, stirring until smooth. Add the prawns and fish, and combine carefully. Remove from the heat and place in an ovenproof dish.
6. Preheat the oven to 180 °C.
7. Make the topping. Mix all the ingredients together and spoon over the filling.
8. Bake until puffed-up and golden. Serve hot.

bliss

DELECTABLE DESSERTS

5

Jenny's Carrot Cake
Serves 10

500 ml (2 c) cake flour
5 ml (1 t) salt
10 ml (2 t) baking powder
7 ml (1½ t) bicarbonate of soda
10 ml (2 t) ground cinnamon
500 ml (2 c) sugar
375 ml (1½ c) oil
4 eggs, beaten
500 ml (2 c) finely grated carrot
250 ml (1 c) canned crushed pineapple, drained
250 ml (1 c) finely chopped walnuts
250 ml (1 c) desiccated coconut
125 ml (½ c) poppy seeds

ICING
125 ml (½ c) butter
250 g package cream cheese
5 ml (1 t) vanilla extract
750 ml (3 c) icing sugar

METHOD
1. Preheat the oven to 180 °C.
2 Combine the first 5 ingredients in a large bowl.
3. Stir in the sugar, oil and eggs. Mix well.
4. Thoroughly blend in the carrot, pineapple, walnuts, coconut and poppy seeds.
5. Turn the batter into a greased and floured 23 cm x 33 cm cake pan or 800 g loaf pan.
6. Bake for 50-55 minutes, or until firm and risen and receding from sides of pan. Cool briefly in the pan, then turn out onto a wire rack to cool completely before icing.
7. To make the icing, first beat the butter until softened, then beat in, in turn, the cream cheese, vanilla extract and icing sugar until smooth.

Rice Cream
Serves 4-6

I nearly married a Greek once, and I was told by his cousin's wife – I think her name was Sylvia – that if I could not make a good rice pudding, I was out. Well, Sylvia, let me tell you it was not my rice pudding he was interested in!

190 ml (¾ c) uncooked rice
1,25 litres (5 c) milk
1 vanilla pod or 5 ml (1 t) vanilla extract
190 ml (¾ c) sugar
10 ml (2 t) cornflour, mixed to a paste with a little cold water
2 egg yolks, beaten
60 ml (4 T) honey, plus extra for drizzling
125 ml (½ c) chopped walnuts
50 g flaked almonds
ground cinnamon

METHOD
1. Place the rice in a large saucepan with the milk and vanilla pod, bring to the boil and cook until rice is tender, about 20 minutes.
2. When the rice is soft, reduce the heat to moderate, add the sugar and mix well.
3. Add the cornflour, and stir until the mixture thickens.
4. Gradually add a little of the rice to the egg yolks and stir well.
5. Pour the egg yolk mixture into the rice and continue to cook over moderate heat until creamy, stirring all the time. Remove from the stove.
6. Place a little honey in the bottom of a small serving bowl, sprinkle with nuts, top with rice cream and dust with cinnamon.
7. Serve hot or cold, drizzled with extra honey, if desired.

Baked Cheesecake with Berry Topping
Serves 6

BISCUIT BASE
85 ml (⅓ c) butter, melted
200 g ginger biscuits, crumbled

FILLING
3 eggs
125 ml (½ c) sugar
500 g creamed cottage cheese
15 ml (1 T) flour
5 ml (1 t) grated lemon zest
125 ml (½ c) cream, lightly whipped

BERRY TOPPING
200 g frozen berries of your choice, half-thawed
125 ml (½ c) castor sugar

METHOD
1. First make the crust. Mix together the melted butter and ginger biscuit crumbs. Press into a 22 cm diameter pie dish and chill until firm.
2. Preheat the oven to 150 °C.
3. To make the filling, first beat the eggs and sugar together until light and fluffy.
4. Gently fold in the cottage cheese, then the flour and lemon zest.
5. Fold in the cream and pour into the prepared biscuit crust.
6. Bake for 45 minutes, or until set, but still slightly wobbly at the centre.
7. Mix together the topping ingredients and spoon over the cheesecake just before serving.

bliss

Coconut Pannacotta
Serves 4-6

2 cardamom pods, split
500 ml (2 c) cream
250 ml (1 c) coconut milk or cream
15 ml (1 T) gelatine
85 ml (⅓ c) sugar
toasted shaved or shredded coconut, or berries, to decorate

METHOD
1. Add the cardamom pods and seeds to the cream and coconut milk. Heat gently until bubbles appear around the edges of the pot. Do not boil! Remove from the heat.
2. Mix the gelatine and sugar together. Add this to the cream and keep stirring until it has dissolved.
3. Pour into individual glasses or bowls or 1 large glass bowl and leave to cool, then cover with plastic wrap and place in fridge to set.
4. Top with toasted coconut shavings or berries.

* Use green cardamom pods as opposed to the white ones, which are blanched green ones. The flavour of the green pods is more intense.

Berry Creams
Serves 1

Make as many as you like. Use home-made yoghurt for this – the taste and texture will stay in your memory bank of sensations forever.

icing sugar to taste
45 ml (3 T) mixed frozen berries
15 ml (1 T) cream cheese
15 ml (1 T) mascarpone cheese
30 ml (2 T) Greek yoghurt
fresh berries, as many as you like

METHOD
1. Mix a little icing sugar with the partially thawed berries.
2. Mix together the cream cheese and mascarpone.
3. Layer the cream cheese mixture and berries alternately in tall, stemmed glasses.
4. Top with Greek yoghurt and fresh berries and serve.

Spicy Apple Sponge
Serves 6

This is just great, served either hot or cold.

3 whole cloves
1 cinnamon stick
250 ml (1 c) sugar
1 piece lemon zest
125 ml (½ c) water or apple juice
6 large cooking apples, peeled, cored and thickly sliced

TOPPING
60 ml (4 T) butter
125 ml (½ c) castor sugar
grated zest of ½ lemon
pinch of sea salt
pinch of grated nutmeg
pinch of ground ginger
2 large eggs
250 ml (1 c) self-raising flour, sifted
165 ml (scant ⅔ c) milk
50 ml (⅕ c) flaked almonds
extra butter for dotting
honey, to drizzle

METHOD
1. Mix together the cloves, cinnamon, sugar, lemon zest and liquid.
2. Cook over moderate heat for a few minutes to dissolve the sugar, then reduce the heat to a simmer.
3. Add the apple slices and poach until tender, about 10 minutes.
4. Remove the apples and place in an ungreased ovenproof baking dish.
5. Preheat the oven to 180 °C.
6. To make the topping, cream the butter, castor sugar and lemon zest together until light.
7. Stir in the salt, nutmeg and ginger.

8. Beat in the eggs, one at a time.
9. When thoroughly incorporated, add the flour by folding it in alternately with the milk.
10. Spoon the mixture over the apples and bake for 40 minutes, or until a skewer inserted in the centre comes out clean.
11. Sprinkle with the flaked almonds, dot with butter and drizzle with honey.
12. Pop under a hot grill for a couple of minutes to brown the almonds lightly. Serve with whipped cream.

Cheat's Cassata
Serves 8-10

Make this a couple of days before you need it.

125 ml (½ c) sultanas
10 red glacé cherries, sliced
5 green glacé cherries, sliced
15 ml (1 T) chopped preserved ginger
2 preserved green figs, thinly sliced
45 ml (3 T) brandy
2 litres vanilla ice cream
100 g toasted hazelnuts, skins rubbed off

METHOD
1. Toss the fruit in the brandy, cover and leave overnight.
2. Next day, remove the ice cream from the freezer and leave at room temperature for about 10 minutes, to soften slightly.
3. Add the fruits and nuts and mix thoroughly with the ice cream.
4. Scoop into a dish, mould or loaf pan and freeze until firm.
5. Transfer from the freezer to the fridge 30 minutes before serving.
6. Unmould, slice and serve.

Honey-buttered Apples and Nuts with great blobs of Vanilla Ice Cream

Serves 4

100 g butter
125 ml (½ c) honey
4 apples, cut into thick rings, skins and core intact
50 g hazelnuts
50 g flaked almonds
50 g pecan nuts
great blobs of vanilla ice cream

METHOD

1. Place the butter in a saucepan and heat it over low heat until it foams and froths.
2. Add the honey and let the mixture bubble like lava. (But take care not to let it burn!)
3. Add the apples and nuts, let it go wild (i.e. cook, uncovered, over moderate heat) until the liquid is reduced and a syrup forms.
4. Divide between serving dishes and serve hot, topped with ice cream and drizzled with a little sauce … then roll it around on your tongue for a great taste sensation.

Pears in Red Wine
Serves 6

The (more or less) traditional way. I usually make two batches: one in white wine and one in red wine. I then halve the pears and serve the red and the white together, with red wine syrup and fresh cream. My family loves these – especially the white wine version, because they think the pears come out of a can!
These pears will keep for a few days, covered, in the fridge.

6 large, firm pears
600 ml (scant 1½ c) red wine
200 ml (⅘ c) sugar
1 cinnamon stick
3 cloves
1 star anise

METHOD
1. Peel the pears leaving the stalk intact, then slice a thin piece off the base of each pear so that it can stand up in the saucepan.
2. Pour the wine into a saucepan large enough to hold the pears in a single layer.
3. Add the sugar and the spices and stir over moderate heat until the sugar dissolves.
4. Increase the heat and bring the wine to the boil. Add the pears, turn down the heat to low and simmer for about 30 minutes.
5. Turn the pears in the wine so that they cook evenly.
6. When the pears are just tender, remove them from the saucepan, using a slotted spoon.
7. Increase the temperature and boil the sauce, uncovered, over high heat until reduced by half. Pour over the pears and serve hot or cold.

Cheat's Pears in Red Wine
Serves 4

This is the quick(er) version.

1 x 825 g can pear halves
375 ml (1½ c) red wine
cloves
1 cinnamon stick
pinch ground ginger

METHOD
1. Drain the pears and reserve 150 ml (⅗ c) of the juice.
2. Place the pear juice, red wine, 3 cloves, cinnamon stick and ginger in a saucepan.
3. Bring to the boil, cover and reduce the heat to a simmer. Simmer for 10 minutes.
4. Stud the pears with cloves. Place in the saucepan and simmer gently for 5 minutes, turning them once.
5. Transfer to a flat bowl and marinate, covered, for at least 24 hours in the fridge.
6. Serve chilled, with fresh cream.

Buttered Pears in Ginger Syrup
Serves 4

This can be whipped up while someone else clears the table. To me, this is a heavenly combination – the sharp saltiness of the blue cheese and the smooth creaminess of the mascarpone with the buttery ginger pears.

4 firm Forelle pears
100 g butter
90 ml (6 T) ginger syrup

MASCARPONE TOPPING
100 g good-quality blue cheese
250 ml (1 c) mascarpone cheese

METHOD
1. Slice each pear lengthways into 3, keeping the stalk intact.
2. Heat the butter in a very large frying pan over moderate heat and add the ginger syrup.

3. Cook until bubbling, then add the pears and cook until just tender. Take the pan from the heat.
4. Mash the blue cheese roughly and fold it, very gently, into the mascarpone.
5. Place the pears in dishes, top with mascarpone topping and serve.

Bread and Butter Pudding
Serves 6

Mom, I'm sorry to say that this version does not remind me of my childhood; but I prefer this one!

100 g butter
125 ml (½ c) honey
2 oranges, peeled and sliced
4 thin slices of day-old bread
2 whole eggs
2 egg yolks
grated zest of 1 orange
30 ml (2 T) castor sugar
350 ml (1⅖ c) cream
2 ml (½ t) ground cinnamon
extra honey
125 ml (½ c) toasted almonds

METHOD
1. Melt half the butter in a large frying pan. Stir in the honey and cook until bubbling.
2. Add the orange slices and cook for 2 minutes.
3. Spoon the oranges and honey sauce into a 1 litre buttered ovenproof dish.
4. Butter the bread slices and cut into triangles. Arrange in a layer over the oranges.
5. Mix together the eggs, egg yolks, orange zest, sugar, cream and cinnamon. Pour over the bread and leave to stand, covered, for 30 minutes.
6. Preheat the oven to 180 °C.
7. Bake for 30-40 minutes, until crisp and lightly browned on top.
8. Remove from the oven, drizzle with honey and sprinkle the toasted nuts over. Serve hot.

Hot Cambrieni in Puff Pastry
Serves 4

1 whole cambrieni, preferably Simonsig
1 roll (400 g) frozen puff pastry, thawed
1 x 125 g jar redcurrant jelly or you can use Glaze n' Baste™ (Medium)
1 x 125 g slice blue cheese
250 ml (1 c) chopped walnuts
1 egg, beaten with water to make an egg wash

METHOD
1. Freeze the cambrieni. Roll out the thawed pastry.
2. Preheat the oven to 200 °C.
3. Place the frozen cheese in the centre of the pastry.
4. Spread the redcurrant jelly over the cheese, and top with the blue cheese and nuts.
5. Enclose cheese by drawing up the pastry edges and forming a twist.
6. Brush the pastry with egg wash, and bake until cooked and golden.
7. Cut into wedges and serve immediately.

Nutty Choc Rusks
Makes 32

1 kg cake flour
10 g instant yeast
200 g sugar
10 ml (2 t) salt
125 ml (½ c) sesame seeds
65 ml (¼ c) sunflower seeds
125 ml (½ c) chopped hazelnuts
125 ml (½ c) chocolate chips
2 eggs, beaten
500 ml (2 c) buttermilk, at room temperature
150 ml (⅗ c) oil

METHOD
1. Mix together all the ingredients (except the eggs, buttermilk and oil) in a large mixing bowl.
2. Gently heat the oil in a small saucepan until lukewarm.

3. Beat together the eggs and buttermilk.
4. Add the oil and stir until well-incorporated.
5. Add the buttermilk mixture to the dry ingredients in the bowl and mix well.
6. Knead for about 10 minutes, or until smooth, elastic and satiny.
7. Let the dough rest on a floured surface for about 5 minutes.
8. Cover with plastic and leave for 20 minutes in a warm place.
9. Knock down the dough and divide into 32 equal-sized pieces shaped into balls.
10. Pack balls into 2 lightly greased loaf pans. Brush with oil.
11. Cover and leave to rise until doubled in size.
12. Preheat the oven to 180 °C.
13. Bake for 40 minutes, or until cooked and receding from sides of loaf pans.
14. Cool slightly in the pans, then turn out and break into rusks (when cool enough to handle).
15. Set the oven to 100 °C and – with the door slightly ajar – dry the rusks, preferably overnight.

Nutty Stuffed Brie and Blue
Serves 8-10

200 g blue cheese
2 x 250 g tubs mascarpone cheese
1 x 1 kg Brie round, preferably Dalewood
100 g walnuts
1 jar Glaze 'n Baste (medium)
citrus leaves, sliced kiwi fruit and fresh berries to decorate

METHOD
1. Cream together the blue cheese and mascarpone cheese.
2. Halve the Brie horizontally. Place the bottom half on a suitable platter (which has enough room to garnish around the cheese).
3. Spread half the creamed cheese mixture onto the bottom half of the Brie and top with half the walnuts.
4. Plonk the other half of the Brie on top of the cheese and nuts.
5. Cover with the remaining creamed cheese mixture, Glaze 'n Baste and remaining walnuts.
6. Garnish around the Brie with citrus leaves, sliced kiwi fruit and fresh berries.
7. Serve with water biscuits.

Choc-tipped Almond Fingers
Makes 24

Great for serving with coffee after a meal. Sandwich them together with mascarpone cheese flavoured with your favourite liqueur; I chose Cointreau.

```
4 egg whites
500 ml (2 c) ground almonds
500 g white sugar
1 ml (¼ t) ground cardamom
grated zest of 1 orange
1 x 250 g slab good-quality dark cooking chocolate
icing sugar for dusting
```

METHOD
1. Preheat the oven to 150 °C.
2. Whisk the egg whites in a very clean, grease-free bowl until soft peaks form.
3. Mix the almonds, sugar, cardamom and orange zest together and, using a metal spoon, gently fold the mixture into the egg whites.
4. Fill a piping bag with the mixture and pipe fingers onto a greased baking sheet.
5. Bake for 10-15 minutes, or until lightly golden.
6. Remove from the oven, then carefully remove the fingers from the baking sheet, using a spatula, and cool on a wire rack.
7. Melt the chocolate in the top of a double boiler, over simmering water.
8. Dip the fingers into the melted chocolate and leave on a wire rack to dry.
9. Dust lightly with icing sugar and serve the fingers.

*   Alternatively, sandwich fingers together with mascarpone before serving.

in-stinct

6

BASIC SECRETS
FOR ALL
FOOD LOVERS

Preserved Lemons

When my lemon tree groans under the weight of all the fruit, I preserve them for later. I just love the oil drizzled over plain cooked rice. This recipe is for my sister, Beverly Perold.

```
8 medium-sized lemons
coarse sea salt
olive oil
garlic
cloves
sliced red chillies
coriander seeds
whole black peppercorns
```

METHOD
1. Quarter the lemons, taking care not to cut them all the way through.
2. Pack sea salt into the cut lemons and close them up.
3. Place the lemons in sterilised jars. Add a few peeled cloves of garlic, some sliced red chilli and a few coriander seeds and some peppercorns to the bottle, top with olive oil, seal tightly and store in a cool, dark place for 8 weeks before using.

* To sterilise jars, wash them thoroughly in hot soapy water, rinse thoroughly, drain and dry on a clean towel. Warm the jars in the oven, preheated to 110 °C, for 20 minutes.

Zesty Olives
Makes 1 kg

Lemon, thyme and garlic on fish, chicken, lamb and with your olives – fabulous! I eat all the lemon bits from the jar first. Then I pop the fleshy green fruit into my mouth, bite into the crisp flesh, suck on the salty juices … then I gnaw away at the flesh. The pip never leaves my mouth until it is sucked clean.

1 kg large green olives in brine
coarsely chopped peel of 6 lemons
a large handful of thyme stems, bruised
6 cloves of garlic, still in their skins, bashed
500 ml (2 c) olive oil
250 ml (1 c) white wine vinegar

METHOD
1. Layer the olives, lemon peel, thyme and garlic in sterilised jars.
2. Add the olive oil and vinegar to the jars, seal and give them a good shake.
3. Store for 10 days before using.

* Whole or sliced chillies can also be added to the olives.

Sour Cream Dressing

Makes 375 ml (1½ c)

1 clove garlic, crushed
250 ml (1 c) sour cream
125 ml (½ c) chopped chives
5 ml (1 t) grated lemon zest
salt and milled black pepper

Mix all the ingredients together.

Red Pepper Sauce

Makes about 300 ml (1⅕ c)

Great on pasta, with as much shaved Parmesan as you can afford!

5 large, fleshy red peppers, roasted (see recipe on page 49) and
    reserving the juices
65 ml (¼ c) olive oil
125 ml (½ c) red wine
1 clove garlic
salt and milled black pepper
125 ml (½ c) torn fresh basil

METHOD
1. Skin the peppers.
2. Place the peppers and their juice, olive oil, wine and garlic in a blender and whizz
   till smooth.
3. Season with salt and pepper.
4. Stir in the basil.

*   Alternatively, you can gently cook everything together, then liquidise and strain it to
    make the sauce.

Cheese Sauce

Makes about 400 ml (1⅗ c)

15 g butter
15 g flour
300 ml (1⅕ c) milk
½ tsp English mustard (optional)
pinch of grated nutmeg
250 ml (1 c) grated cheese of your choice
salt and milled black pepper

METHOD
1. Melt the butter in a saucepan over moderate heat.
2. Add the flour and cook, stirring, for 1–2 minutes.
3. Remove from the heat when the mixture begins to bubble.
4. Add the milk gradually, stirring all the time.
5. Return the saucepan to the heat and cook, stirring all the time, until the sauce begins to thicken, about 2 minutes.
6. Stir in the mustard and nutmeg, then the cheese. Stir till cheese has melted. Don't let the sauce boil.
7. Add salt and pepper to taste and use at once.

Sweet Pastry Crust

Makes 1 tart shell

100 g butter
250 ml (1 c) cake flour
45 ml (3 T) castor sugar
1 egg yolk

METHOD
1. Fling the butter, flour and sugar into a food processor, and give it a few whizzes until it resembles fine breadcrumbs.
2. Add the egg yolk and blitz the mixture a few times until it just comes together. Don't overwork the pastry.
3. Wrap in plastic wrap and let it rest in the fridge for 1 hour.
4. Roll out the pastry on a floured surface and use as desired.

Home-made Yoghurt
Makes 600 ml (2⅖ c)

This yoghurt is really versatile. We eat it for breakfast with fruit; I add chillies, garlic and coriander and serve it with curry; or I add mint and garlic and serve it on meat balls. Lastly, it is rich and creamy served as a dessert, oozing with honey and nuts.

600 ml (2⅖ c) long-life skimmed milk
210 ml (14 T) skimmed milk powder
15 ml (1 T) plain live yoghurt – read the label; if it is not really live, it won't work

METHOD
1. Heat the milk until it is tepid. Do not overheat the milk, as this will kill the culture.
2. Add the skimmed milk powder and yoghurt and whisk the mixture until well-blended.
3. Warm a glass bowl with boiling water, then pour in the yoghurt mixture.
4. Cover with foil to keep in the warmth, wrap in a towel and place in a nice warm spot. Leave it undisturbed for 6–8 hours, or until it is set.
5. Once the yoghurt has set, put it in the fridge where it will thicken nicely.
6. Always save a tablespoon of the yoghurt to make your next batch; the yoghurt gets thicker and better each time you make it.

Herby Vinaigrette
Makes 250 ml (1 c)

60 ml (4 T) red wine vinegar
5 ml (1 t) brown sugar
salt and milled black pepper
2 cloves garlic, crushed
15 ml (1 T) chopped fresh mint
5 ml (1 t) chopped fresh rosemary
5 ml (1 t) chopped fresh oregano
180 ml (12 T) extra-virgin olive oil

METHOD
1. Shake everything together, except the olive oil, so that the sugar and salt can dissolve.
2. Add the olive oil and give the dressing a good shake to mix.

* One variation I really love consists of 3 parts olive oil, 1 part lemon juice and 10-15 ml (2-3 t) honey shaken to combine with lots of shredded mint and crushed garlic. This also makes a great marinade for lamb.

Mayonnaise
Makes about 400 ml (1⅗ c)

What do you want it to be? See suggestions after the recipe for ways to use this extremely versatile mayonnaise. And make your own mayonnaise just once, to taste the difference!

2 egg yolks
30 ml (2 T) lemon juice
salt and milled black pepper to taste
5 ml (1 t) English mustard
375 ml (1½ c) virgin olive oil

METHOD

1. Place your egg yolks in a glass bowl, add the lemon juice, salt, pepper and mustard, and whisk together until well-blended.
2. This next part is rather like foreplay: slowly add the oil, drop by drop, beating all the time, until a quarter of the oil has been absorbed.
3. Now you can really get down to business! Add the remaining oil in a steady stream, beating continuously until everything is combined.
4. Adjust the seasoning, if necessary.

* Verjuice, lime juice or white wine vinegar can be used instead of lemon juice.
* You can whisk by hand, or use something electric – like a blender or food processor.

Where do you want to use it?
Just add one of these:
30 ml (2 T) chopped capers (use for fish)
15 ml (1 T) chopped fresh dill
15 ml (1 T) grated lemon zest
freshly chopped parsley, chives, tarragon, basil, coriander, or rocket
creamed horseradish
crushed garlic
mashed anchovies (great with eggs)
chopped olives
crumbled blue cheese
chopped walnuts
boiled eggs
I've run out of space - now you take the recipe and own it!

Garnishes

Frosted fruit, flowers and herbs:
Dip grapes or redcurrants into whisked egg whites, drain lightly and toss in a bowl of castor sugar until completely covered. Place on a rack in a warm, dry place to set and harden.

Here are a few edible flowers:

MARIGOLDS

PANSIES

VIOLETS

NASTURTIUMS

ROSES

VIOLAS

BORAGE

CALENDULA

CAMOMILE

ZUCCHINI (BABY MARROWS)

HOLLYHOCKS

LAVENDER

MINT LEAVES AND FLOWERS

BERGAMOT LEAVES AND FLOWERS

CLOVE CARNATIONS

WHITE JASMINE

ELDERFLOWERS (GREAT WITH GOOSEBERRIES)

ROSEMARY LEAVES AND FLOWERS

FENNEL LEAVES AND FLOWERS

* A word of caution – do not use any of these if they have been sprayed with pesticides or insecticides.

When I'm with my garden, my vegetables and herbs, I think of life and relationships:

THYME – what we must always make for each other.

ROSEMARY – for friendships. How can you be a lover if you can't be a friend? You need to like before you love.

LAVENDER for tranquillity, roast lamb and headaches.

ROCKET – what you get up your bottom for being slack. Also for salads, pasta, and cheese sandwiches.

MINT – for how fresh your breath should smell when you open your eyes. Also wonderful with peas, fruit and lamb.

BAY LEAF – You can bay as much as you like, but I'm still not in the mood! Also good in stews, pickles and curries.

CARROTS – what you get for not doing your bit. Also full of carotene, and good for you!

GARLIC, my fragrance for life.

CELERY – what you need to survive; also great in soups.

SPRING ONION – I am not one any more. Remember to eat the whole thing.

MULBERRY – That's how I'm known. Makes a great sauce for duck and game, as well as a wonderful jam.

FIG – What I don't give if you don't like my food – naked or cooked – once you've had one, you're hooked.

love
letters

RECIPES

FROM

FRIENDS

Schiacciata della Vendemia
Sweet dough tart with harvest grapes
GENNARO CONTALDO, PASSIONE RESTAURANT, LONDON
Serves 4-6

Gennaro Contaldo, the London "father" and mentor of Jamie Oliver the Naked Chef, is a wonderfully warm and generous friend with a sense of humour from hell. He's the devil in disguise, naughty and ever so nice, and I'm honored to have him in my book and cannot wait to cook with him again. Gennaro, you are an inspiration to everyone who knows you.

"It is traditional in Italy at harvest time to put aside some grapes to consume at Christmas. The grapes become deliciously sweet and squashy and make a perfect filling for a pie. My family always conserved grapes on the vine and with them would make this tart, using leftover bread dough. I am not suggesting you should conserve grapes to make this tart, as nowadays you find them all year round. Use the sweet varieties of grapes such as Moscatel or Hanepoot, or ask your greengrocer. This is a lovely, unusual pie, perfect at teatime."

20 g instant yeast
165 ml lukewarm water
300 g bread flour
6 g salt
breadcrumbs
450 g black grapes
75 ml (5 T) extra-virgin olive oil (45 ml [3 T] for filling & 30 ml
  [2 T] for topping)
60 g sugar (50 g for filling & 10 g for topping)
15 ml (1 T) ground cinnamon
1 rosemary sprig

love letters

METHOD

1. Dissolve the yeast in the lukewarm water and set aside.
2. Sift the flour into a large bowl, mix in the salt and make a well in the centre. Add the yeast mixture gradually and mix with the flour to make a soft dough (same consistency as for making bread).
3. Remove from the bowl, and knead on a clean, floured surface for about 10 minutes. Divide the dough into 2 balls. Cover the dough with a cloth and leave to rest for 5 minutes.
4. Preheat the oven to 200 °C.
5. Roll 1 ball out into a round shape, about 2 mm thick and 15 cm in diameter, using a rolling pin.
6. Sprinkle a large baking sheet with breadcrumbs and gently place the round base on it.
7. Take the grapes (leaving about 4–5 aside) and place on the dough, leaving about 2.5 cm free all around.
8. Drizzle 45 ml (3 T) of the olive oil over. Sprinkle 50 g of the sugar and all the cinnamon on top.
9. Sprinkle the rosemary needles over.
10. Roll the other dough ball out as described and place this over the filled base, pressing the edges down well. Trim away any excess pastry. Using your fingers, press the dough and fold it over (like a Cornish pasty) so that the pie is well sealed and the filling cannot escape during cooking.
11. Drizzle the remainder of the olive oil over the top and sprinkle with the remaining sugar.
12. Bake for 20 minutes. Halfway through cooking, place a small bunch of about 8–10 grapes with some sprigs of rosemary on the top of the pie and continue to bake.
13. Remove from the oven and decorate with icing sugar. Delicious served warm at teatime.

Il Ragu
Filled beef rolls slow-cooked in tomato ragu
GENNARO CONTALDO, PASSIONE RESTAURANT, LONDON
6 servings

This dish takes me back to my childhood Sunday lunches, and to family gatherings when I return to my home village. My Aunt Maria was the "Queen" of this dish and would spend all morning checking, stirring and making sure it was just right for all the family to enjoy. The dish is known as Il Ragu and is traditionally made each Sunday by most families in all regions in Southern Italy. It is a simple dish to prepare and takes about 2 hours to cook – some traditionalists will cook it for longer to get an even richer tomato sauce, but if you follow this recipe, 2 hours will suffice. The tomato sauce is used to flavour pasta for the primo (pasta course) and the meat is eaten as a main course. And, of course, any leftover sauce can be used to flavour pasta dishes throughout the week.

12 small sirloin steaks, thinly sliced
salt and milled pepper
30 g Parmesan cheese, grated
4 garlic cloves, finely chopped
a handful of fresh flat-leafed parsley, torn
90 ml (6 T) olive oil
150 ml (⅗ c) red wine
1 onion, peeled and very finely chopped
1 celery stick, very finely chopped
30 ml (2 T) tomato concentrate, diluted in 400 ml (1⅗ c) lukewarm
  water
2 x 400 g cans chopped tomatoes
a handful of fresh basil, torn

METHOD
1. Arrange the meat on a chopping board or a clean work surface and flatten the steaks with a meat mallet – if you don't have one, place a flat wooden spatula over the meat and bash with the palm of your hand.
2. Season each piece of meat with salt and pepper, and sprinkle with grated Parmesan cheese, chopped garlic and parsley. Roll each slice up tightly and secure with toothpicks.
3. Heat the olive oil in a large saucepan. When hot, reduce the heat, add the meat rolls and seal well on all sides. Increase the heat, add the red wine and cook until the wine has half-evaporated. Remove the pieces of meat and set aside.
4. Add the onion and celery to the pan and stir well. Cook until the remainder of

the wine has nearly evaporated and the onion begins to sweat. Return the meat to the pan, add the diluted tomato concentrate and the chopped canned tomatoes. Season with salt & pepper, add the fresh basil, and stir well. Reduce the heat, cover with a lid (not completely, so some of the steam can escape) and cook for 2 hours, stirring from time to time. Check for seasoning.
5. Serve the tomato sauce with cooked fresh pasta such as tagliatelle or large rigatoni. Then serve the meat rolls as a main course with a green salad.

Roasted Figs scented with Thyme
ERRIEDA DU TOIT
Serves 6

Errieda, a woman, a friend who shares my passions and pleasure in food.

Sweet purple-cheeked figs, swollen with glorious juices and tender flesh, are sensual symbols of summer. The best way to enjoy them is fresh, slightly chilled. If you are blessed with an abundance of summer figs, this recipe will have you swooning with delight.

2 ripe, but firm figs per person
10 ml (2 t) fresh thyme leaves

SYRUP
60 ml (4 T) orange blossom honey
50 ml (⅕ c) unsalted or low-salt butter
1 cinnamon stick
sweet wine

METHOD
1. Make deep cuts into the blossom end of the figs, without cutting right through. Place in an attractive oven dish.
2. Preheat the oven to 180 °C.
3. To make the syrup, put the honey, butter, cinnamon stick and sweet wine in a small saucepan and heat until liquid.
4. Pour the honey syrup over the figs and bake for 12–15 minutes.
5. Remove from the oven and sprinkle the thyme over the figs. Switch off the oven and return the figs to the oven for another 5–7 minutes.
6. Serve at room temperature with dollops of thick Greek yoghurt.

* Sprinkle with roasted pine nuts or pistachio nuts for a more intense flavour.

Grilled Steak Salad with Buttermilk and Mustard Dressing

FRANÇOIS FERREIRA

My wonderful, mad friend François, we have worked on so many things together; we have laughed, cried, screamed and danced together, not forgetting how we have cooked together. I do so love you!

MARINADE
100 ml (⅖ c) soy sauce
50 ml (⅕ c) oil
15 ml (1 T) grated fresh ginger
2 cloves garlic, crushed

4 x 200 g sirloin, rump or ostrich steaks
1 packet mixed lettuce leaves
1 onion, peeled and sliced
1 small English cucumber, thinly sliced

DRESSING
100 ml (⅖ c) buttermilk
1 clove garlic, crushed
15 ml (1 T) whole-grain mustard
30 ml (2 T) olive oil
salt and milled black pepper to taste

METHOD
1. Mix the marinade ingredients and marinate the steak for about 1 hour.
2. Preheat a steak pan and pan-grill the steak as desired. Remove from the pan and allow to rest for about 15 minutes, then slice into strips.
3. On a platter arrange the lettuce, onion rings and cucumber decoratively.
4. Lastly, arrange the strips of steak on the platter.
5. Mix all the dressing ingredients together and sprinkle over salad. Serve immediately.

Beetroot and Porcini Mushroom Risotto
PATRICK WERKX, PATIO GENK, BELGIUM
Serves 4

My wonderful friend for life.

1 litre (4 c) chicken stock
500 ml (2 c) water
250 ml (1 c) dry white wine
30 ml (2 T) olive oil
30 g butter
200 g porcini mushrooms
2 cloves garlic, crushed
4 spring onions
500 ml (2 c) uncooked risotto rice
2 uncooked beetroot, peeled and cubed
20 g flat-leafed parsley, roughly chopped
10 g fresh basil, torn
440 g pancetta, chopped
Parmesan shavings to flavour and garnish

1. Bring the stock, water and wine to the boil in a medium-sized saucepan.
2. Reduce the heat, cover, and keep hot.
3. Heat the oil and butter in another saucepan. Cook the mushrooms, garlic and spring onions until tender.
4. Add the rice and beetroot.
5. Add 250 ml (1 c) stock and bring to the boil, stirring until the stock has been absorbed by the rice. Reduce heat if necessary.
6. Continue adding the stock in the same way until all the stock has been absorbed and the rice is creamy, about 35 minutes.
7. Remove from heat and add the freshly chopped parsley and basil.
8. Pan-fry the pancetta until crisp. Place the risotto on plates and garnish with crisp pancetta and Parmesan shavings.

White Chocolate Crème Brûlée
FRANC LUBBE, RESTAURANT ZERO 932, CAPE TOWN
Serves 6

I like the dessert flashed under a hot grill and chef Franc prefers a blow job – I mean using a blow torch, of course – but do whatever you prefer. It wasn't easy getting this recipe out of Steven and Franc. At one stage I thought I might have to use a blow torch on them to get them to let go!

I hope you enjoy the brûlée as much as their thousands of diners have. The best part, I find, is breaking the caramel top with a hard whack, sinking your spoon into the creamy delight that awaits you beneath, and then just to let your mouth fall in love with you again …

1 litre (4 c) cream
240 g castor sugar
120 g white chocolate
1 vanilla pod
12 egg yolks

METHOD
1. Scald the cream with the castor sugar, white chocolate and vanilla pod until the chocolate melts. Allow to cool to room temperature.
2. Mix in the egg yolks.
3. Pass the mixture through a sieve.
4. Divide between 6 ramekins and place in a baking tin with high sides. Pour in sufficient water to come halfway up the sides of the ramekins.
5. Preheat the oven to 150 °C.
6. Bake the desserts for about 1 hour, then remove from the oven.
7. Check if the brûlée has a jelly-like consistency, then refrigerate for 3 hours. If it doesn't have a jelly-like consistency, leave it in the oven for a little longer.

* For dinner parties, it would be best to make the creams early in the morning.
* Make sure the cream doesn't boil while you are scalding it; if it does, the dessert could split while you bake it in a bain marie (water bath).
* Enjoy with a sexy chick on a languid summer's evening.

Pagnotta Pugliese
MICKI CIMAN, LA MASSERIA RESTAURANT, DURBANVILLE
Makes 2 loaves

Tables groaning with food, Lorenzo serenading the guests … Kiki, Nona and Paola … Gnocchi di Patate served with sage and burnt butter, light and fluffy topped with Parmesan shavings … then there are the beautiful purple artichokes … Oh, Micki, how you spoil me! The voluptuous, luscious, purple figs split open and eaten naked, I'm talking about the essence of the fig, now, although I'd have no problem sitting down naked in front of an overflowing bowl of figs, bringing the bowl to my face and taking in their perfume, then sinking my teeth deep into the flesh. And the long lunches; now you're not allowed to leave until the last drop of wine touches your glass, and that can be forever. But the bread, I'm forgetting about the bread – don't get started on the bread, or you will never get to the groaning table.

1 kg cake flour
10 ml (2 t) salt
10 g instant yeast
about 1 litre (4 c) lukewarm water

METHOD
1. Sift the flour into a large mixing bowl (remember, the dough will double in volume) and make a well in the centre.
2. Sprinkle the salt and the yeast around the well. Pour in half the water and mix from the inside of the well. Pour in the rest of the water gradually, adding just enough to make a soft, elastic dough. Always add the water under the dough (not poured on top) and knead well for about 10 minutes.
3. Sprinkle flour over the dough and cover with a tea towel. Rest in a warm place away from draughts until it has doubled in size, about 1 hour.
4. Flour a working surface on your working table and place the dough on it. Divide in two and shape into a round, like a large bun. Don't handle the dough too much as it will lose the air.
5. Flour a baking sheet large enough to hold 2 loaves and place them side by side on it, making sure there is some space between them. Cover the loaves and leave them to rise for 25–30 minutes.
6. Preheat the oven to 220 °C.
7. Bake the loaves for 20 minutes, then reduce the temperature to 180 °C and bake for a further 20 minutes.
8. Remove from the oven and place in a basket or on a cooling rack until cool.

love letters

* This bread will keep fresh for at least 3 days if you keep it wrapped in a cloth and away from draughts. As the bread gets older, it is absolutely delicious for bruschetta. Buon appetito!

Ryan's Pancake Mix
Serves 6

Our children may irritate us when they get under our feet in the kitchen, especially after a long, hard day. But we should be patient, and encourage them – if they have the passion we could be shaping their future. What I did was put the kids in the corner with a block of rock-hard frozen butter and a cup of sugar, a wooden spoon and a large bowl and said to come back to mom when it's creamy. The other skill is the knife skill: the neck of a butternut and a plastic knife keeps them quiet for hours. Ryan has been cooking from the age of 10 – he cooked on two Gourmet Festivals and two Waterfront Food Fairs. I used to think I was his only mentor, but this has changed over the years, as he has sent faxes to Alan Coxon asking questions, spending holiday and weekend time in the kitchen with Enzo Cocca, making pizzas, right up to firing in the pizza oven. He is now 12, and the passion grows daily.

3 eggs
250 ml (1 c) sugar
500 ml (2 c) cake flour
250 ml (1 c) milk
10 ml (2 t) baking powder
10 ml (2 t) vanilla essence
butter for frying

METHOD
1. Beat the eggs and sugar until fluffy. Add the flour and milk to the eggs and beat well.
2. Stir in the baking powder and vanilla essence.
3. Heat a little butter in a frying pan and fry 1 spoonful of batter at a time, turning once to cook on both sides. The size and number of spoonfuls you use will depend on the size of your frying pan.

How to eat it
Serve the pancakes topped with dollops of mascarpone cheese or vanilla ice cream, topped with fresh berries and drizzled with honey.

"Sex on a Spoon"

ALAN COXON, COXON'S KITCHEN COLLEGE, UK
Serves 6

Alan Coxon, we all thought you were a goody-goody. Watch his eyebrow to see what I mean … A warm and sincere friend, loved by me and my whole family. It's a pleasure having you on my pages. This dish gives me goose bumps.
You will need a tall, fluted 1,25 litre (5 c) pudding mould as well as butter for greasing and castor sugar for dusting.

100 g plain chocolate
6 extra-large free-range eggs, separated
2 ml (½ t) ground cinnamon
100 g castor sugar
100 g chopped almonds
50 g soft fresh breadcrumbs

METHOD
1. Melt the chocolate in the top of a double boiler over simmering water, then beat it with the egg yolks, cinnamon and half of the sugar until it is foamy.
2. Mix the almonds with the breadcrumbs and set aside.
3. In a grease-free bowl, and with a grease-free whisk, whisk the egg whites until a peak is formed.
4. Gradually add the remaining sugar, whisking continuously, as if making meringues.
5. Using a metal spoon, blend about a quarter of this meringue into the egg yolk mixture, then carefully fold in the breadcrumb and almond mixture.
6. Finally, fold in the remaining egg whites.
7. Preheat the oven to 160 °C. Grease the mould and dust with sugar.
8. Carefully fill the mould with the mixture.
9. Stand the mould in a baking tray and pour in enough warm water to reach to about 2,5 cm below the rim of the mould. Bake for 35–40 minutes, making sure the water remains just under boiling point.
10. When ready, turn out from the mould and pour over some lightly whipped cream and lashings of chocolate sauce.
11. At this point, ensure that the curtains are closed; then, finally, gently insert your spoon into the dessert, removing a mouth-sized portion, with a generous quantity of the sauce and cream. Savour the mouth sensation … then swallow!

Jewelled Coriander Fish
LANNICE SNYMAN
Serves 4-6

My friend the fishwife – I have to call her that, because if I call her the doyen of fish and all things culinary, she will fillet me. Lannice has been an inspiration for as long as I can remember. She has taught me an awful lot about fish, and I have collected every one of her *Sunday Times* recipes and every book she has published. Love you, Lannie.

This boldly flavoured fish dish is one my favourites from *Free From The Sea*, my very first cookbook, published in 1979, and still going strong. It's got great texture and goes brilliantly with garlic mash or pasta tossed with a dash of olive oil. Any white fish is good (as long as it's fresh as fresh can be) but my favourites are game fish such as tuna or yellowtail, or more delicately flavoured kingklip, geelbek or red steenbras.

800 g fish fillets
salt and milled black pepper
flour
5 ml (1 t) coriander seeds, lightly crushed
80 g butter
30 ml (2 T) olive oil
300 g small pickling onions, skinned
125 ml (½ c) good-quality wine vinegar
250 g cherry or Rosa tomatoes
45 ml (3 T) sultanas

METHOD
1. Cut the fish into cubes, season with salt and pepper and dredge with flour.
2. Roast the coriander in a dry, non-stick frying pan until aromatic and lightly browned – watch it carefully as it's quick to burn. Set aside.
3. Heat the butter and olive oil in the same pan and fry the fish cubes until they are nicely browned and just cooked through. Remove the fish from the pan and set aside.
4. Add the onions to the pan and brown quickly.
5. Add the vinegar and coriander, and season with salt and pepper. Cover and cook gently until the onions are tender but still quite crisp, then add the tomatoes and sultanas.
6. Cook, uncovered, over high heat for 1–2 minutes, or until the sauce thickens slightly.
7. Return the fish to the pan and heat through, then transfer everything to a serving dish.

The Best-ever Banana Cake, studded with Chocolate and Raspberries
ABIGAIL DONNELLY, FOOD EDITOR, *FAIR LADY* MAGAZINE

Abigail, I love working with you – your sense of humour, your patience and flair go a long way in my book. (Excuse the pun, which, of course, is intended.)

250 ml (1 c) castor sugar
65 ml (¼ c) brown sugar
250 ml (1 c) mashed banana
125 g butter, melted
3 eggs
190 ml (¾ c) sour cream
440 ml (1¾ cup) self-raising flour
75 g dark chocolate, roughly chopped
190 ml (¾ cup) raspberries

METHOD
1. Preheat the oven to 180 °C.
2. Mix together the sugars, banana, butter, eggs and sour cream until smooth.
3. Add the flour and stir to combine.
4. Spoon the mixture into a medium, greased loaf pan and push the pieces of chocolate and the raspberries into the dough.
5. Bake for 40 minutes or until a skewer inserted into the centre comes out clean.

Uccelli Scappati
ENZO COCCA, MONELLO'S RESTAURANT, CAPE TOWN
Serves 2

Ravenous is not the word for what I feel when I set my foot inside my friend Enzo's restaurant, Monello's. The aroma of fresh bread baking, and the sweet spicy smells of succulent, fleshy red peppers and fennel roasting, drive me crazy. It's hard to leave and go back to my own kitchen, my dearest Enzo, I do so appreciate you.

2 large chicken breast fillets, sliced
salt and milled black pepper
6 sage leaves
2 slices Parma ham
30 ml (2 T) olive oil
30 ml (2 T) butter
1 lemon, halved
65 ml (¼ c) white wine
1 bunch wild or ordinary rocket
extra olive oil for drizzling

METHOD
1. Pound the chicken slices until thin and the same thickness. Season with salt.
2. Press 2 torn sage leaves onto the chicken.
3. Lay a slice of Parma ham on each breast.
4. Roll the breasts up from the narrow end and cut each in half.
5. Thread onto a large skewer, securing loose ends.
6. Heat the olive oil and l5 ml (1 T) butter in a frying pan, over moderate heat.
7. Place the skewer in the frying pan, with one half of the lemon, flesh side down.
8. Brown the chicken evenly on both sides and cook through. Remove from the pan.
9. Add the white wine and the remaining butter to the pan and cook rapidly, uncovered, to reduce. Add the remaining sage leaves.
10. Place washed rocket to the side of a plate. Place the roasted lemon in the centre and place the skewer on other side. Dress with the reduced pan juices.
11. Squeeze the juice from the remaining lemon half over the rocket and drizzle with olive oil.

glossary

À la Means 'in the style of' in French.

Absorption method Cooking rice by adding the exact quantity of water and cooking with the lid on until all the water has been absorbed and steam holes appear in the surface of the rice.

Acidulate To add acid (such as lemon juice or vinegar) to cooking or soaking water to stop fruit or vegetables from oxidising and discolouring.

Additive Something added to food to improve its keeping qualities, flavour, colour and texture. In the European Union, all additives are listed by e numbers or names on packaging, unless they are natural and therefore not required by law to be listed.

Adjust To taste before serving and add more seasoning, if necessary.

Aerate To incorporate air into a mixture by sifting dry mixtures or whisking liquid mixtures (such as egg whites or cream).

Aged balsamic vinegar Concentrated, complex balsamic vinegar from Modena in Italy, bearing the words, aceto balsimico tradizionale di modena.

Aioli Powerful garlic mayonnaise, used on hot or cold boiled fish, stirred into fish soup or melted over green vegetables and boiled potatoes.

Al dente Until just cooked. Refers mainly to pasta, rice and vegetables.

Al', all alla Means 'in the style of' in Italian.

All-purpose flour American term for plain white flour that can be used for all types of baking.

Anticaking agent Something added to powdered food to stop its clumping together, usually a compound of magnesium, aluminum or sodium. Shown as an e number on packaging (e530–e578).

Antioxidant A preservation agent, such as vitamins C or E, that slows the reaction rate of food to oxygen. Shown as an e number on packaging (e300–f321).

Apéritif Drink, such as sparkling wine or sherry, taken before a meal to "open" the appetite.

Appellation d'origine French designation for a wine or foodstuff.

Appetiser Small items of food served before or at the start of a meal, or with drinks.

Aromatics Ingredients, such as spices and herbs, that add aroma to food.

Aspic A savoury jelly; any finished cold dish that includes this jelly, e.g. ham in aspic.

Au gratin Browned under the grill; usually has a covering of crumbs and butter.

Aubergine A purple, white or purple and white streaked vegetable used extensively in Provençal and Greek cooking. Also known as eggplant or (in SA) brinjal.

Baby marrow Also known as courgette or zucchini.

Bake To cook in an oven in dry heat, usually until browned on the outside.

Bake blind To bake an unfilled pastry case to set the pastry. The pastry is usually lined with baking paper/parchment or foil and filled with baking beads to stop the sides collapsing or the base from bubbling up. If baking beads aren't available, use dried beans or raw rice.

Baste To spoon melted fat, wine, stock or liquid over food as it cooks to stop its drying out and to add flavour.

Batter A mixture of flour, milk and eggs used for pancakes and to coat food before frying. Also refers to soft cake, biscuit and scone mixtures.

Beat To incorporate air into a mixture with a spoon, fork or whisk.

Beurre manié Equal quantities of flour and butter made into a paste and whisked into a boiling liquid to thicken it without making lumps.

Blend To mix together until thoroughly incorporated. Nowadays this may mean in a liquidiser, blender or food processor.

Blue Very rare meat, which is still raw at the centre.

Bocconcini Means 'mouthfuls' in Italian, but is usually applied to small balls of mozzarella.

Bone To remove bones from a bird or piece of meat, leaving the flesh intact.

Bouquet garni Flavouring for soups and stews, usually made from a bay leaf and sprigs of parsley, thyme and marjoram tied together with string.

Broil American word for grill.

Broiler American word for a young chicken.

Broth The liquid in which meat, fish or vegetables and flavourings have been cooked. Also refers to a clear soup.

Brown To cook food until the outer surface turns brown, usually to seal in the juices in meat. Also called searing (q.v.).

Bruise To crush lightly. Used for aromatics like lemon grass to ensure they will release their flavour more easily.

Buffalo mozzarella Italian-style mozzarella cheese made from buffalo milk.

Cannellini beans Small, white, dried beans.

Capsicum *see* Sweet peppers

Caramelise To heat food until the sugars on the surface break down and form a brown coating, which may be sweet or savoury. Also, to heat sugar until it turns light brown.

Clarify To skim or filter a liquid until it is clear, or to add beaten egg whites over heat, which then coagulate and trap any impurities.

Coating consistency A liquid that is thick enough to coat food evenly without running off again. Test by pouring over the back of a spoon; a line drawn down the centre of the spoon should hold its shape.

Cold-pressed oil Oil that is extracted by pressing but without being heated or having any chemicals added. Cold-pressed oils have a better flavour.

Core To remove the inedible centres and seeds of fruits. Also refers to removing the blood vessels and tubes from a kidney.

Coriander A popular herb, also known as cilantro and dhania.

Coulis A thick, sieved sauce, usually of tomatoes or fruit.

Courgette Also known as baby marrow or zucchini.

Cream To beat ingredients to incorporate air and make the mixture creamy in consistency.

Crust A pastry case such as a pie crust, or the browned surface of baked goods such as bread or cakes.

Cube To cut food into blocks about 2,5 cm square. Cubes are larger than dice.

Dark soy sauce A dark, rich sauce that has fermented longer than light soy sauce. Used for colour and flavour.

Devein To remove the dark, vein-like digestive tracts from prawns, shrimps, langoustines and crayfish.

Dice To cut into tiny cubes.

Dot To scatter or put small pieces of butter over the surface of food before cooking.

Dough A mixture of flour, liquid and other ingredients that form a pliable mixture used for making bread.

Dredge To dust with a powder such as icing sugar or flour.

Dressing A mixture of oil and vinegar used to dress salads.

Drizzle To sprinkle liquid in a continuous stream.

Dropping consistency When a mixture will fall slowly off a spoon, i.e. it won't run off or stay put.

Dry-fry To cook food in a frying pan without any added fat (oil, butter, lard etc.).

Dry-roast To heat spices in a frying pan over high heat, without added oil, to improve their flavour.

Dust To sprinkle lightly with a powder such as icing sugar, flour or cocoa.

Egg wash A glaze made from eggs and water or milk. Used in baking.

Essence Concentrated flavour derived from an ingredient, usually by macerating in alcohol.

Extract Concentrated flavour derived from an ingredient, usually by distillation or evaporation.

Fat-free If a food item is labelled fat-free, the total ingredients should contain less than 0,5 g fat per 100 g.

Fold in To mix two mixtures together, using a gentle lifting and turning motion rather than stirring, so as not to lose any trapped air bubbles. Used for cake mixtures and when adding flavourings to meringues.

Fry To seal the surface of food quickly by cooking it in hot fat.

Garam masala A blend of spices originating in North India, based on varying proportions of cardamom, cinnamon, cloves, coriander, fennel and cumin, roasted and ground together.

Ginger juice To make, finely grate a piece of ginger, place in a muslin or cloth and squeeze juice into a small bowl.

Glacé(e) Frozen (iced) or glazed.

Glaze A coating applied to a surface to make it shine or to help it colour when cooked, such as an egg wash for uncooked pastry and an apricot glaze for fruit tarts.

Grease To coat a dish, pan or mould with cooking fat in order to stop the item being cooked from sticking.

Haloumi A firm, chewy cooked sheep's milk cheese (it can also be made from cow's milk) that originated in Cyprus. Usually matured in brine. It tastes a little like feta cheese and should be fried or grilled, then served immediately before it becomes rubbery.

Hand-hot Or 37 °C – the temperature at which a liquid feels neither hot nor cold. Also known as blood temperature, or lukewarm.

Hard-boil To boil an egg until both the white and yolk are set (about 9–10 minutes from start of boiling).

Harissa A fiery paste from North Africa, usually made from fresh or dried red chillies, garlic, dried coriander and mint, caraway seeds, fresh coriander, salt and olive oil.

Hull To remove the stalks from berry fruit.

Infuse To soak something in a hot or warm liquid (such as tea) in order to transfer flavour, colour and aroma to the liquid, which is later strained.

Julienne To cut food into fine sticks, thinner than matchsticks or shreds.

Jus Cooking juices or light stock served as a sauce.

Knead To mix a stiff dough by manipulating it by hand or with a mechanical dough hook in order to make it smooth. In bread-making, this also helps to develop the gluten.

Knock back/down To knead gas bubbles out of a yeast-risen dough.

Lard To thread strips of lard through a lean piece of meat in order to baste it as it cooks.

Leavening agent A substance, such as baking powder or yeast, which adds volume in the form of gas bubbles and lightens the texture of baked goods.

Liaison A thickening agent for a sauce, soup or stew made from eggs and cream, or starches such as arrowroot. A liaison is added at the end of cooking.

Light soy sauce Saltier and lighter in colour than dark soy sauce.

Line To add a protective coating such as greaseproof paper (cake pans), strips of bacon, thin slices of cake (for charlottes) to a dish in order to stop a filling sticking or to contain a soft filling.

Liquidise To break down to a purée in a blender or food processor.

Lite (light) A term that simply means a food has less of something. It is used to describe things such as fat, flavour, colour, sugar, alcohol and kilojoules and is not governed by any regulations. For example, lite oil is light in flavour and colour, not fats or kilojoules.

Low in fat, low-fat Products labelled "low in fat" in the USA, and European Union guidelines, must have less than half the fat of a full-fat version (exact levels are set by legislation). "Low-fat", however, can mean anything that has slightly less fat than the full-fat version.

Macerate To soak food in a liquid so that it absorbs the flavour of the liquid. Often used to describe soaking in alcohol and sugar syrup.

Mange-tout Waxy peas in pods, called sugar snap peas in Britain. The whole thing including the pod is eaten.

Marinade A collection of liquid flavourings in which foods are soaked so they take on the flavour; and, sometimes, to tenderise. Many marinades include an acid such as fruit juice (to tenderise the food) and an oil.

Marinate To soak food in a marinade.

Mascarpone A fresh, unripened cream cheese resembling thick clotted cream, with a rich, slightly acidic, sweet taste.

Pan-fry To fry in a frying pan in a small amount of fat.

Parboil To half-cook something in boiling water.

Parmigiano reggiano Parmesan cheese made by traditional methods within a defined area in Italy and aged for at least 18 months.

Pâté A cooked paste of meat, poultry or fish, either set in a terrine or cooked in pastry.

Pipe To force a mixture through a nozzle, either smooth or patterned, in order to cover or decorate a surface or make an exact shape.

Poach To cook gently in a barely simmering liquid.

Pomodoro A thick, Italian-style tomato sauce.

Porcini Dried Italian mushrooms, also known as ceps or boletus mushrooms. Available from delicatessens and some supermarkets. To use, soak in hot water for 15 minutes, drain, then chop, reserving the liquid for stocks or casseroles.

Pouring cream Also known as fresh or pure cream. It contains no additives and has a fat content of 35 percent.

Praline A blend of toasted almonds (or, sometimes, other nuts) and caramelised sugar.

Preserved lemon Lemons preserved in salt and lemon juice; a North African speciality.

Primavera An Italian term that denotes the use of spring vegetables.

Prove To allow a yeasted dough to rise; also to heat a frying pan or wok with oil or salt and then rub the surface, thus filling in any minute marks with the mixture and making it nonstick.

Provençale, à la Denotes the use of tomatoes, garlic and oil among other typical ingredients from Provence.

Pulp The flesh of fruit and vegetables, or the matter left behind when fruit or vegetables have had all their juice extracted.

Purée A fine, soft, almost pourable paste made by processing or pounding food.

Quiche Savoury open tart, almost always with egg as part of the filling. The fillings served without pastry (i.e. in a gratin dish) are called gratins.

Rare A steak that has been cooked for a short time and is still pink inside.

g l o s s a r y

Reduce To boil a liquid rapidly, uncovered, in order to remove water by evaporation. This thickens the liquid and intensifies the flavour.

Refresh To put just-cooked items into ice-cold water in order to stop them cooking further, as well as to prevent loss of colour and texture.

Rehydrate To add water to something that has been dehydrated to plump it out again.

Rest For meat, to set aside to allow the juices to settle (about 10–15 minutes for a whole roasted chicken or a leg of lamb). For batter, to set aside to allow starch to swell for a lighter result. For pastry, to set.

Roast To cook in an oven at a high temperature without any covering in order to give a crisp, well-browned exterior and a just-cooked, moist interior. Usually applied to meat, poultry or vegetables, though anything can be roasted.

Roux A mixture of flour and fat cooked together and then used as a thickening agent, e.g. in sauces and soups.

Rub in To integrate hard fat into flour by rubbing the two together with your fingertips until the mixture resembles breadcrumbs.

Saffron threads Threads from the dried stigmas of the crocus flower. Available from delicatessens and some supermarkets,

Sambal ulek (sambal) Indonesian chilli paste made from pounded chillies, salt, vinegar or tamarind (oelek).

Scald To immerse in, or pour over, boiling water for a short time in order to cook only the outer layer. Also, to bring milk almost to the boil; or to sterilise kitchen equipment in boiling water.

Sear To brown the surface of meat in hot fat before cooking it fully.

Season To add flavouring, usually salt and pepper, to bring out other flavour in a dish.

Sell-by date The date by which food must be sold. The food is not necessarily inedible on this date, but will not last much longer.

Shallots Also known as eschalots or French shallots. Small, teardrop-shaped, golden brown bulbs that grow in clusters.

Shelf llfe The length of time a product will stay fresh.

Shortening The fat used in baking. The term refers to the ability (shortening power) of the fat to allow the mixture to trap air bubbles and make it light.

Shred To cut food into very thin strips.

Sleve or **sift** To aerate and remove any lumps from a dry powder such as flour or icing sugar.

Simmer To maintain a cooking liquid at a temperature just below boiling point.

Skim To remove fat or scum from the surface of a liquid using a large spoon, ladle or skimmer.

Slake To mix a powder, such as cornflour, with a little liquid to form a paste that can then be mixed into a larger quantity of liquid without forming lumps.

Soft-boil To boil an egg until the white is just set and the yolk is runny (about 4–5 minutes).

Spanish onion A large, purplish-red onion with a mild flavour. Also known as red onion.

Sponge A bubbly, batter-like mixture made by mixing flour, yeast and a liquid and allowing it to stand for several hours. The first step in some bread-making recipes. Or to soak gelatine in a liquid until absorbed.

Steam To cook in the steam given off by boiling or simmering water.

Steep To infuse.

Stew Meat cooked by the circulation of water. It is therefore always cooked on top of the stove so that the liquid is free to move around.

Stir-fry To cook pieces of food quickly in a wok using only a little oil and moving them around constantly.

Stud To insert flavourings such as whole cloves (into an onion) or slivers of garlic (into a piece of meat) into a piece of food before cooking.

Sweat To cook in fat over low heat without letting the food brown.

Sweet peppers Also called bell peppers or capsicums. Remove the seeds and membranes before use.

Tahini Sesame seed paste.

Tamarind Soft dried pulp of the tamarind pod.

Tenderise To break down the tough fibres in flesh by mechanical (pounding), chemical (acid) or natural (hanging) means.

Terrine Chopped or ground meat (sometimes, though rarely, fish) baked in a terrine dish. A terrine is always served cold.

Top and tail To remove the stalks and tips from fruit and vegetables.

Toss To mix a dressing through food, usually a salad, so that it becomes coated. Also means to shake pieces of meat in flour to coat them; or to turn food in a pan by flipping it out of the pan.

Trim To remove unwanted bits from meat or fish, or to cut something to a specific shape.

Truss To hold something, usually meat or poultry, in shape with string or skewers while it cooks.

UHT (ultra heat treated) Liquid that has been heated quickly and cooled quickly to sterilise it.

Unleavened Made without any raising agents.

Verjuice The unfermented juice of unripened grapes, with a delicate lemon/vinegar flavour.

Whip To incorporate air into something by beating it (cream, egg white) with a whisk or to form an emulsion by the same means (mayonnaise).

Zest The very finely peeled rind or outer layer of citrus fruit, which contains the essential oils.

Zucchini Also known as baby marrows or courgettes.

Oven Temperature Conversion Table

Celsius	Fahrenheit	Gas mark	Oven
50	120	¼	
70	160	¼	
100	212	½	
110	230	½	Very cool
130	265	1	
140	285	1	
150	300	2	Cool
170	340	3	Moderately cool
180	355	4	Moderate
190	375	5	Moderately hot
200	390	6	Hot
220	430	7	Very hot
230	445	8	
240	465	8	
250	480	9	Extremely hot
270	520	9	
290	555	9	

Weights Conversion Table

US/UK	Metric	
1 oz	30 g	
2 oz	60 g	
4 oz	125 g	¼ lb
5 oz	155 g	⅓ lb
6 oz	185 g	
7 oz	220 g	
8 oz	250 g	½ lb
10 oz	315 g	
12 oz	375 g	¾ lb
14 oz	440 g	
16 oz	500 g	1 lb

index